DIGGING THE TRUTH:
The Final Resting Place of Jimmy Hoffa

DIGGING FOR THE TRUTH:
The Final Resting Place of Jimmy Hoffa

JEFFRY SCOTT HANSEN

SPECTRE PUBLISHING

DETROIT

2009

SPECTRE PUBLISHING
Detroit, Michigan

Copyright © 2009 Jeffry Scott Hansen
All Rights Reserved

First printing September 2009

Front & Back Cover © 2009 Spectre Publishing
Designed by Heather Hansen
Interior photos used by permission

No part of this book may be reproduced
or transmitted in any form or by any
means without written permission from
the publisher. For information
regarding this book or other Spectre
Publishing titles visit our website at
www.spectrepublishing.com

Library of Congress Control Number:
2009902523

ISBN 13: 978-0-9709191-6-8
ISBN 10: 0-9709191-6-6

Printed in the United States of America

Acknowledgements

This book has my name on the front cover, but would not have become a reality without the encouragement and help from several people.

I would like to thank:

-My beautiful, fantastic wife, Heather, for all of her input and help and for all of the times I had to drop what I was doing to take a phone call or travel to various meetings or locations during this project. Thank you for your editing, patience, and suggestions, you are the best.

-My daughters, Deborah, Anna, Margaret, and Erin, for understanding when I had to chain myself to the computer to write this book.

-My grandfather, Edward DeCourcy, who instilled in me the investigative spirit and drive to seek the truth in this case.

-My mother, Margaret, for all her enthusiasm.

-My aunt Janette DeCourcy for putting me in contact with Monty Wulff of Charles R. Step Funeral Home in Redford, Michigan.

-My brother, Technical Sergeant Joseph Hansen USAF.

-My lifelong friend, Marty Sigarto, and his wife Maria, who took time off work to help me videotape the drive to Grand Lawn Cemetery on June 2 2006.

-To my fellow police officers led by Chief of Police Dale Tamsen and especially:

-Commander Don Helvey for all of his support and knowledge of this case and organized crime. He was with me every step of the way, and I greatly appreciate all his help.

- Detective Maureen Brinker for the information regarding forensics, and her husband, Corporal Bill Brinker, for all of his encouragement.

-Corporal Damon Smith and his wife, Sarah, and her parents, Robert and Marcia Terrazas, for their help regarding Jimmy Hoffa's Lake Orion home.

-Ray Prall, current owner of the Hoffa cottage in Lake Orion, Michigan for allowing access to his property.

-Rick Wilson and his wife, Helen, for their time and recollections and access to their home on Beaverland Street in Detroit.

-Dennis Barger, my friend and media agent, for all his work behind the scenes and for helping me contact the FBI Agent in Charge of the Hoffa File.

-Kevin Siembieda, Alex Marciniszyn, Wayne Smith, Julius Rosenstein, Jason Marker, and Kathy Simmons of Palladium Books, for being my friends and proofreading my book.

-Monty Wulff of Charles R. Step Funeral Home, Redford, Michigan for his recollections and information.

-Mr. Ellis of Ellis Funeral Home on Grand River Avenue, Detroit.

-*Detroit Free Press* Reporter Dave Ashenfelter for putting me in contact with Charles Brandt.

-Reporter Joel Thurtell, also of the *Detroit Free Press*, for writing the first article to bring Grand Lawn and Evergreen Cemetery to the public's attention.

-Jerry Lynott of the *Times Leader* newspaper in Wilkes-Barre, Pennsylvania.

-Jason Richards for creating the interior map for this book. Visit his website *www.jasonrichards.net*.

-All of the other investigators of this mystery, especially Dan Moldea and Steven Brill, for the dangerous work they were involved in during the preliminary stages of the Hoffa investigation.

-Scott M. Burnstein, author of *Motor City Mafia: A Century of Organized Crime in Detroit*, who gave me some very useful information about the Detroit Outfit.

-Eric Shawn of the Fox News Channel for his thoughts about the case and his help in spreading the word about this new information.

-My friends at the City of Warren: Joe Cochran, Adam Bullis, Justin Crown and the crew at *TV Warren*. You guys are awesome and I am proud to be a part of your team.

-Bob and Janet Baker for allowing Charles Brandt and me into their home and answering our questions.

-Jeff Sturm and Denaca Stabnick for their valuable input and proofreading.

-Jerry Stanecki, the newshawk from *WXYZ TV* Detroit for his recollections about the case.

I want to recognize Grand Lawn Cemetery in Detroit for allowing me access to the grounds, the Holden Chapel Mausoleum, and the cremation logs and records of Holden Chapel Crematorium. Their willingness to allow this research for historic value has given me the factual basis to support the main theory of how Jimmy Hoffa was killed and how his remains were disposed in 1975. Without access to

Grand Lawn, the investigation of Evergreen Cemetery would have never happened.

- Ole Lynklip and Arthur Stickles and the staff at Evergreen Cemetery for all of their help and cooperation during this investigation.

From the Author

I would like to begin this book with sincere condolences to the family of James R. Hoffa. For the past thirty-four years, they have had to bear the rumors, jokes, and media circus to what must be the most horrible event a family could ever go through. I cannot express in words how sorry I am for their loss.

This book will begin with background about Mr. Hoffa and his rise to power. It will end with the discoveries I have made over the course of three years.

Frank Sheeran's confession to Charles Brandt, author of *I Heard You Paint Houses: Frank "the Irishman" Sheeran and the inside story of the Mafia, the Teamsters, and the last ride of Jimmy Hoffa* (Steerforth Press, 2005) brought to light many details of Mr. Hoffa's death and disappearance. No other person that close to Jimmy Hoffa had ever given such a detailed account of not only Hoffa's disappearance, but of the world of the Teamsters and its relationship with organized crime. The facts I gathered for this book have led me to believe that a cemetery in Detroit is the final piece of the puzzle surrounding the whereabouts of Mr. Hoffa's body.

This book is dedicated to:

Charles Brandt,
A great friend, finder of fact and seeker of truth. Your expertise in this case has been an enormous help and I am eternally grateful for your belief in what was discovered during my investigation.

The Hoffa Family,
May you all find closure to this tragedy.

James R. Hoffa,
One of the greatest labor leaders of all time. Sir, may you finally rest in peace.

Preface

Jimmy Hoffa.

For people alive in the 1950's and 60's, this name was one of power. It was synonymous with the American working-man, labor, and union. There is no doubt that under Hoffa's control, the *International Brotherhood of Teamsters* became the most influential union in the world. At its height of power the Teamsters had almost two-million members and encompassed working class jobs from truckers to warehousemen, longshoremen, and contractors. Several books have been written about the history of the Teamsters, which existed as a union long before Hoffa, but it did not enjoy the clout or power it would know until he took the reins of leadership.

Before Jimmy Hoffa became the most famous missing person since Amelia Earhart, he was a force with whom to be reckoned. He was notorious for his negotiations with trucking companies and heated verbal battles with Robert Kennedy during Senate Hearings. During the golden age of television, those public confrontations made him a household name with the likes of Ed Sullivan and Elvis Presley.

Most Americans under the age of thirty have heard of Jimmy Hoffa, but do not know the real story behind the man. One of their few references is the 1992 movie *Hoffa* which is loosely based on his life and completely fictionalizes his murder. For several years I have been interested in this case. After all, I was born and raised in a working class neighborhood in Northwest Detroit. My Grandfather was a truck driver and Teamster, making Mr. Hoffa's whereabouts a common discussion around our dinner table. We often saw news reports on the *CBS Evening News*, and television shows, like *In Search Of,* reference the famous labor leader and his infamous disappearance.

I have been asked many times why is Jimmy Hoffa such a big deal and why would anyone still care what happened to him after all these years. There are several reasons. First, he was so powerful that with a single phone call he could shut down just about every trucking company, warehouse, and shipyard operating in the United States.

Second, this man stared down big business and the U.S. Government on a daily basis and never flinched. He helped change the way businesses deal with their employees and contracts. Thirdly, and most importantly he was somebody's son, husband, father, and brother. People tend to forget about his family, when they discuss his notoriety and the mystery surrounding his death. His daughter, retired Judge Barbara Crancer, and his son, current Teamster's President James P. Hoffa, have sought closure on their father's death for several decades.

Local, State, and Federal authorities have also continued to investigate this case for the last thirty-four years. Millions of dollars have been spent in the many attempts to locate Mr. Hoffa's remains and put those responsible for his death behind bars.

The Jimmy Hoffa case is one of those topics on which many people have an opinion or theory. It has become a pop-culture sensation and because of that, it has been one of the most difficult murder investigations of the twentieth century. Hollywood and Late Night Talk shows continue to make fun of Mr. Hoffa's disappearance, murder, and purported location of his body in movies like *Bruce Almighty* and on television programs like the *Tonight Show*.

One might get the impression that I admire Jimmy Hoffa and his fight for the working class, and as you read this book, it will be apparent that I do. However, I will also be the first to say that the people Mr. Hoffa allied himself with were some of the most ruthless, self-serving and dangerous people of the criminal underworld. In doing so, he allowed himself to become corrupted. The men he called friends would ultimately be his undoing. A working class hero or ruthless mafia influenced union boss, Jimmy Hoffa will always be remembered as the tough Teamster from Detroit and a tragic figure of history.

James Riddle Hoffa

The story of Jimmy Hoffa began on February 14, 1913, in Indiana. Jimmy's father, John, died when he was seven and four years later, his mother Viola, moved Jimmy, and his siblings to southwest Detroit. At that time, thousands of workers from all over the country travelled to Michigan in hopes of finding a good job and living "the American Dream".

In the 1920's, children living in the shadow of Detroit's auto industry grew up too fast. Financial instability and a lack of child-labor laws forced the Hoffa children to adapt in order to survive. Historians reference Viola Hoffa as a tough-as-nails, no-nonsense, hard-working woman. This trait rubbed off on her children, especially Jimmy.

In order to help support his family, Jimmy took a job as a delivery boy for a west side grocery store. His day-to-day routine included walking to the Frank C. Neinas School, doing homework and going to work. By ninth grade, he had dropped out. Times were tough, and the 1929 stock market crash made life even tougher. While in his teens, Jimmy worked the warehouses where trucks and railcars would deliver fresh produce for grocery stores. As a dockworker, Jimmy made thirty-two cents an hour unloading crates of produce for the Kroger Food Company. He performed backbreaking work, which rarely allowed rest during exhausting twelve-hour shifts.

Work began in the late afternoon where he and the other men would wait, often without pay, for shipments to arrive. If there were no deliveries, the men received no pay. However, if they chose to leave the yard, they would lose their job.

One of Hoffa's foremen was a tyrant who browbeat the workers for no reason and fired them just because he could. Men like this were commonplace. They enjoyed playing God to those who could not fight back and epitomized the term bully.

For Jimmy Hoffa, these men and the companies they represented, were a catalyst for his negative opinion toward the world of corporate America and its relationship with the working man.

With conditions so poor, and pay even worse, Jimmy Hoffa was fed up with the treatment he and the other men were receiving. One warm spring night, under Hoffa's lead, they demonstrated their disgust by throwing down crates of fresh strawberries on the Kroger docks, and would not load them into the refrigerated train cars. When a foreman promised to take the men's grievances to management the next day, the men resumed loading the strawberries.

The strawberry strike forced Kroger into negotiations with the men to avoid the loss of the produce. Eventually, the workers demands for higher wages and better working conditions were met. Shortly after the strike, Hoffa was fired for accidently dropping a crate of vegetables. Teamsters organizer Ray Bennett noticed Jimmy's attitude towards management and recruited him to become a union organizer. It would be Jimmy's job to bring new blood into the union.

Jimmy Hoffa hit the streets, alleyways, pubs, and warehouse yards to sign men up. The working man was the backbone of the country, and he was going to be the working man's backbone. Arrested several times on picket lines and during brawls with corporate hoods, Jimmy would find himself also fighting police officers who were on the payroll of the companies he was trying to unionize. His mission was not pleasant, but his contempt for corporate America made it a necessity. Companies would fight tooth and nail to keep organizers like him away from their workers and businesses. The problem for those companies was that Jimmy Hoffa would fight back. His time in the streets and all the punch-ups with the cops and goon squads only made him tougher and more resilient. Several fire bombings were attributed to the Teamsters back in the 1930's. The message sent to the laundry and trucking companies was clear: Cause trouble for men wanting to join the Teamsters or for those helping them sign union cards, and your company will suffer the consequences. With these and many other roadblocks, the Teamsters and the unionization of the American working-man did not happen overnight. According to Hoffa, *it took years*.

For Hoffa, the picket line became the office and during a laundry workers' strike in 1936 he met his future wife, Josephine Poszywak. A year later, the two travelled to Bowling Green, Ohio to be married. In 1938, Josephine gave birth to their first child, Barbara, and later in 1941, their second child James P. Hoffa was born.

Early in his career as a Teamster, Hoffa developed a reputation that spread throughout Detroit and the Midwest. Since businesses of the day were not shy to use hired muscle to quell the unionizing of their work force, Jimmy Hoffa, according to several accounts, was compelled to align himself with members of organized crime to counter them.

From 1937 to 1957, as Hoffa rose to the top of the Teamsters, government investigators believed he drew more power from his alleged connections to the mafia. Forming an alliance with Russell Bufalino, Hoffa was deep in the rackets involving everything from pension fund skimming, to extortion and murder. He admitted to a reporter that union bosses who did not use the underworld for muscle were fools. Jimmy Hoffa needed that *muscle* to deal with problems stemming from union infighting and rival unions who were attempting to steal away membership from the Teamsters. Hoffa's muscle came from Russell Bufalino in the form of Frank "the Irishman" Sheeran. Frank became Hoffa's East Coast connection, making himself available to solve delicate union matters.

The fight for power, the alleged firebombs, mob involvement, and murders sent loud signals to federal law enforcement officials. One of the biggest opponents of the hate and discontent born out of the labor rackets in the late 1950's was Robert Kennedy. Before his appointment as Attorney General, he was the Chief Counsel for the McClellan Committee, which targeted the labor movement and its cohabitation with organized crime figures. Hoffa became a focus of the investigations of the committee when he became General President of the Teamsters, in 1957. The back and forth questioning by Robert Kennedy and other members of the committee was national news and was seen by millions of Americans watching on television. (See Appendix)

After failing to get Hoffa indicted during those hearings, Robert Kennedy would have other chances to produce evidence to get Hoffa convicted of a crime.

Robert Kennedy's determination ultimately landed Hoffa in jail in 1967. Hoffa served five years in prison before President Nixon pardoned him in 1971. Hoffa gave up the Teamsters Presidency and appointed Frank Fitzsimmons to take his place. Though he was a free man, a condition of no union involvement until 1980 was placed on Hoffa's pardon. Hoffa, as defiant as ever, planned a come back and began fighting the pardon's unprecedented stipulation and restriction. Up until the day he disappeared, he had a lawsuit pending that would reverse the pardon's conditions.

According to several published accounts, organized crime figures were concerned that Hoffa was going to cooperate with Senate hearings regarding Operation Mongoose, the plot to kill Cuban dictator Fidel Castro and the JFK assassination.

Meanwhile, Hoffa threatened to go public with information about the Teamsters Pension fund and how it was being misused by Frank Fitzsimmons and organized crime. Hoffa was warned that it was not in his best interest to run for the Teamsters presidency, but he would not listen. The plot to kill him was hatched sometime in 1974.

On July 30, 1975, Hoffa left his Lake Orion, Michigan home at approximately 1:15 pm. After driving to the offices of Airport

Service Lines in Pontiac, he drove to Bloomfield Township.

Near the intersection of Telegraph and Maple Road, he waited in the parking lot of the Machus Red Fox for a 2:00 pm meeting with reputed mobsters Anthony Provenzano of New Jersey and Anthony Giacalone of Detroit. At approximately 2:30 pm, Hoffa was observed getting into a four-door sedan occupied by three men. The vehicle left the restaurant parking lot and headed south on Telegraph Road. Hoffa was never heard from again.

The day after his disappearance, local law enforcement as well as the FBI and Michigan State Police began a nationwide manhunt for his whereabouts. Over thirty years later, Jimmy Hoffa remains missing and presumed dead.

Hoffa Cottage
Lake Orion, Michigan

Hoffa, the Government, and The Mafia

In January 1957, the McClellan Hearings opened with the intent to bring to light the infiltration of organized crime into the labor movement. The hearings would bring indictments of racketeering and illegal union activity against former Teamster President, Dave Beck, and his successor Jimmy Hoffa. Hoffa was called to those hearings and the dialog between him and Robert Kennedy became legendary.

As depicted in the 1992 movie, *Hoffa* starring Jack Nicholson, the union boss and Kennedy disliked each other from the beginning. One story has the two rivals arm wrestling at a February 19, 1957 dinner set up by Teamster's lawyer, Eddy Cheyfitz. Hoffa would brag for years to various newspaper reporters that he easily beat Robert Kennedy without a struggle.

In March, the FBI filmed Jimmy Hoffa handing an envelope containing two-thousand dollars to a lawyer named John Cheasty, in exchange for information about the McClellan committee. What Hoffa did not know was that Cheasty had become a counter spy for Robert Kennedy. Hoffa was arrested and charged with bribery. During the trial, celebrities like former heavyweight boxing champion Joe Louis came to the courtroom to show support for Hoffa, even though Joe Louis had no personal relationship with him. Because the jury in the bribery case was two-thirds African-American, Hoffa's primary lawyer Edward Bennett Williams hired an African-American female lawyer, Martha Jefferson, (who happened to be dating Joe Louis at the time), to sit at the defense table. Williams' tactics worked and Hoffa was acquitted of the bribery charges.

In August, during the televised McClellan Hearings, it was obvious that Hoffa could not stand the questioning by a "snot-nosed kid" like Robert Kennedy. In Kennedy's eyes, Hoffa was just another thug taking advantage of the working class families he was supposed to be protecting. By December, Beck and at least twenty other individuals in the union were found guilty. Jimmy Hoffa escaped conviction and his power grew substantially even as the Teamsters were ousted from the AFL-CIO union. Over the next two years, his increasing power brought Hoffa greater trouble.

In September 1959, after 1,525 sworn witnesses and more than 500 hearings produced 46,150 pages of testimony, Robert

Kennedy resigned as Chief Counsel of the McClellan Committee. His brother John's campaign for President of the United States needed his help. When John F. Kennedy was elected president in 1960, Robert was appointed Attorney General. Furious that Hoffa had been acquitted in the bribery trial and that nothing substantial had come from the McClellan Hearings; Robert Kennedy vowed he would put Hoffa behind bars in the near future. He formed the "Get Hoffa Squad" and authored the book *The Enemy Within* based on the investigations of the McClellan Committee.

In 1961, the head lawyer on the Get Hoffa Squad, Walter Sheridan, received information from disgruntled Teamster business manager, Edward Grady Partin. Attorney General Robert Kennedy's luck had turned around. According to Partin, Hoffa was enraged at being indicted for jury tampering, this time in Nashville, Tennessee. He ranted about how "Bobby Kennedy needed to be taken out." It was Partin's surprise testimony, as an informant, that helped land Hoffa's conviction in 1964 for jury tampering in Chattanooga, Tennessee.

To understand Hoffa's contempt for the government, one must understand his personality. He was known for his temper and

was not one to keep his mouth shut. If he had misgivings, he made them perfectly clear. His tirades were legendary and his subordinates knew better than to ever attempt to calm him down or to question his directives. Despite his temper, Hoffa had a very strong, loyal work ethic. In an interview filmed from his office at the Teamster Headquarters in Washington D.C., a reporter asked what he liked to do in his free time. Jimmy Hoffa's answer was that he enjoyed more than anything in the world, was to be at his desk, working for his union members. He was the working-man's union president, someone who looked out for the little guy. As a family man, he always called home when he would be late and never drank alcohol or smoked cigarettes. He frowned upon men who would stay out all night. When he was away on business, he made certain those joining
him were well aware of his standards.

Hoffa saw himself as an equal, if not a superior, to politicians like the Kennedys. John Kennedy was close to the "Rat Pack", a group of Hollywood royalty that included Frank Sinatra, Dean Martin, Jerry Lewis, Peter Lawford, and Sammy Davis Jr. Frank Sinatra was allegedly tied to organized crime with associations to mob boss Sam Giancana of the Chicago Outfit. One of the most shocking allegations regarding JFK, but unproven, was that Giancana and John Kennedy shared the same mistress, Judith Exner. Peter Lawford, John Kennedy's brother-in-law, supposedly facilitated many of John's sexual escapades with many other women, including several Hollywood starlets. While the Kennedy government had spies prying into Hoffa's union activities, Hoffa allegedly had his own spies watching the moral and ethical misdeeds of both Kennedy brothers and others in the government.

Thanks to his own underworld connections, Hoffa had wiretaps and eavesdropping bugs planted in key places where President John Kennedy would have his way with young women. There is speculation that Hoffa even had Marilyn Monroe's bedroom bugged and her phone tapped. Through this very small grapevine, it was learned that she was having sex with President Kennedy and later, Robert. These same audio recordings are purported to have captured the death of Marilyn Monroe in June 1962. The night she died, Attorney General Robert Kennedy was said to be staying on a ranch with his wife Ethel near Gilroy, California. However, several sources reference him being in Los Angeles with Peter Lawford, that very night. The common story was that Monroe overdosed, but evidence, other than the recordings, has pointed to murder. It is speculated that the Kennedy's needed Monroe silenced regarding their alleged affairs and her knowledge of national security matters. One would think Hoffa's knowledge and evidence of these events would have surely made their way to the press. According to persons close to Hoffa, the sex tapes were too sick for public consumption. He did not want to embarrass Jackie Kennedy and her children. If these tapes did exist, they never surfaced. They have either been stolen or confiscated by government agents, so the story goes. There was another reason Hoffa did not reveal the content. He was aware that there were other plans in the works to deal with the Kennedy brothers.

Bring in the Mafia

Jimmy Hoffa's position was often a high-wire act. He was being heavily investigated, with evidence of his alleged crimes piling up. He had already made a name for himself in the McClellan Hearings when Russell Bufalino sent him up-and-coming hit man Frank "The Irishman" Sheeran. Frank was established in Bufalino's turf as a man who could be trusted to take care of delicate matters. He took orders without question, handling jobs with military precision. Sent to Detroit's Teamsters Local 299, Frank would become Hoffa's close ally, committing criminal acts against union dissenters on his orders.

In addition to running the Teamsters, according to Charles Brandt's book, Frank Sheeran claimed that Hoffa was secretly involved in plans to overthrow the Cuban government, which was known as the Bay of Pigs Invasion. The mafia wanted the island country, only ninety miles off the coast of Florida, to go back to its casino resort status. With their hands in the pot, Sam Giancana, Carlos Marcello, Russell Bufalino, Santo Trafficante, and Hoffa could continue making money without U.S. Government intervention.

Frank Sheeran verified the mafia's involvement in the 1961 Bay of Pigs Invasion. At the request of Jimmy Hoffa and Russell Bufalino, he drove a truck to a cement company near Baltimore, Maryland. Carlos Marcello's pilot, David Ferrie, was waiting with soldiers to load the truck with supplies and weapons.

Frank drove to a dog-racing track outside of Jacksonville, Florida. He delivered the weapons to E. Howard Hunt of the CIA. Shortly thereafter, the Bay of Pigs Invasion became an international fiasco. Operation Mongoose, the attempted assassination of Cuban Dictator, Fidel Castro, was also a failure. Hoffa and notorious Cosa Nostra figures were involved, acquiring intelligence and arms for the mission. When it failed, they felt they were left holding the bag.

These situations made the Kennedy brothers some extremely dangerous enemies, not only in Cuba, but also in their own country. The Joint Chiefs of Staff were not happy with Kennedys' appeasement of the Soviet Union during the Cuban Missile Crisis and Fidel Castro was definitely not happy that they were actively trying to kill him. The mafia bosses that had helped the U.S. Government in World War II, as well as providing the logistical support needed to murder a foreign leader were furious and felt double-crossed.

Because of their discontent, key members of Cosa Nostra set plans in motion. Frank Sheeran told author Charles Brandt that in November of 1963, Jimmy Hoffa asked him to report to Russell Bufalino. Bufalino instructed Sheeran to go to Monte's Restaurant in Brooklyn, to meet with Tony Provenzano. Sheeran was given a package to deliver to the same cement company in Baltimore, Maryland.

According to Sheeran, the package was a duffle bag containing at least three rifles. He transported the duffle bag and met again with David Ferrie. A few days later, on November 22 1963, President John F. Kennedy was assassinated. Years later, Hoffa told Frank those very rifles were used in Dallas, specifically for the hit on JFK. They were needed because the original driver, who was drunk, crashed the delivery car, and the weapons were confiscated. As reported in the Dallas Morning Star on November 18, 1963, the actual crash was the result of a high-speed chase with Dallas Police. Nine days before the assassination of JFK, two men, connected to gun-running, were arrested. The intended use of the weapons found in that Thunderbird, and the men's associations to organized crime, is unknown. In 1995 this information surfaced again when JFK researchers Ray and Mary LaFontaine wrote the book *Oswald Talked*, and is still disputed even today.

Dan Moldea, in his book *Hoffa Wars* per a conversation with James P. Hoffa, claims that Jimmy Hoffa knew Jack Ruby. If that is true, it lends credence that organized crime was complicit in the assassination of President Kennedy. Several books debunk the connections as they relate to Hoffa and the JFK assassination, saying that organized crime would not have had the audacity to attempt such a high profile murder.

Other authors suggest that organized crime and Hoffa were planning to kill the President, but that lone assassin Lee Harvey Oswald beat them to it. There is evidence that suggests the murder of JFK at the hand of the mafia was going to take place in Miami, Florida but that the plan was scrapped at the last minute.

While the entire world was mourning the murder of JFK, two infamous statements were uttered. While being questioned by reporters about Kennedy's death, Nation of Islam spokesman, Malcolm X, referred to the murder as *chickens coming home to roost*. Jimmy Hoffa, in front of a Nashville, Tennessee television audience, stated "Bobby Kennedy is just another lawyer now". Malcolm X was censured by his leader, Elijah Mohammed. Hoffa, with no one to answer to, maintained his uncaring attitude towards the Kennedys, coming off as extremely brash to the public. Robert Kennedy's first reaction to the news of his brother's murder was to ask Get Hoffa Squad member, Walter Sheridan, to look into links between Hoffa and the assassination. His gut instinct told him that organized crime and Hoffa were somehow involved. If the assassination was intended to stop Robert Kennedy's prosecution of Hoffa and organized crime, it failed. Hoffa was convicted and sent to prison in 1967.

In June of 1968, Robert Kennedy met the same fate as his brother. Speculation was that elements of the government and organized crime were working hand in hand to take him out before he was able to gain the Presidency. Allegedly, when the news of Robert Kennedy's death reached Jimmy Hoffa in prison, he was quoted as saying "*They* got him!"

On one hand, Hoffa seems to have been a staunch working class hero and family man, and a hard-nosed demagogue and mafia collaborator on the other. That is why it is completely understandable that to this day, he is still both admired and vilified.

Russell Bufalino

Born September 25, 1903 as Rosario Alberto Bufalino in Sicily, Russell Bufalino would become one of the most powerful mafia leaders in the history of organized crime. He was also one of only a handful of Cosa Nostra leadership to survive being the boss for more than four decades. His life was full of intrigue, and though it was never proven, he was implicated in orchestrating both the JFK assassination and the Jimmy Hoffa disappearance/murder.

Those two events alone are enough to keep researchers busy with the thousands of documents and files regarding the mysteries surrounding them. Given the importance of these two cases, and their apparent connections, Russell Bufalino's reach goes further than one would think with just a cursory glance. The web that would grow into Cosa Nostra was spun, surprisingly, by a small group of men like Bufalino who controlled every vice and racket imaginable. In what Robert Kennedy would call the American Organized Crime Syndicate a *second government within a government*, Russell Bufalino was the equivalent of a high-ranking Senator, or Governor.

His rise to power mirrors that of other such underworld figures, from small time criminal acts like petty theft and the fencing of stolen goods to high profile hits of rival gangsters.

As a young man Bufalino would ally himself with the likes of Giovanni Montana, aka John C. Montana, and Joseph Barbara of the Northeastern Pennsylvania crime family. In 1940, when Barbara became head of the family, Bufalino was named as underboss and moved to Kingston, Pennsylvania.

Jimmy Hoffa became President of the Teamsters in 1957, the same year as the infamous Apalachin, meeting. New York City mob boss Vito Genovese, through Buffalo, NY crime boss Stefano Magaddino, called for a meeting with every Cosa Nostra chief in the United States, Canada, and Sicily. On November 14 1957 more than one-hundred members of this secret society met at Barbara's house in New York State. Russell Bufalino helped organize the conference and even secured hotel rooms and food for his partners in crime. At this meeting the men had a sit down regarding events that had affected their organization.

Notable guests included Carlo Gambino, Paul Castellano, and Joseph Profaci of New York City, as well as Santo Trafficante from Florida. The four would be among almost sixty Cosa Nostra crime figures (including Russell Bufalino) that were caught at the meeting by the New York State Police. The other forty or so men eluded police by fleeing into the woods.

Many of the attendees that were arrested had to appear before the Select Committee on Improper Activities in the Labor or Management Field, also know as the McClellan Hearings in Washington D.C. in 1958. The mobsters had to
answer questions as to their purpose for the meeting. Most of those questioned plead the Fifth Amendment to avoid self-incrimination.

While in power, Bufalino's turf was northeastern Pennsylvania, all the way up to

Buffalo, New York and parts of New Jersey. He was so powerful and respected that when the Five Families in New York City needed an acting boss for the Genovese Family, their choice was Russell Bufalino. He was the boss they turned to when problems needed to be handled delicately, as in, to not appear to have come from New York. He was a member of the mafia's so called *commission* and had at his disposal hundreds of henchmen who were stone cold killers. Bufalino was a family man, much like the fictional character Don Corleone of *The Godfather*, but far more ruthless and calculating.

Over the course of thirty years Bufalino was a close ally of Jimmy Hoffa and helped the Teamsters boss consolidate his power in the union. It was Russell Bufalino who dispatched Frank "The Irishman" Sheeran to assist Hoffa in his criminal endeavors, and several years later, sent the Irishman to *dispatch* Hoffa to keep him from regaining control of his beloved Teamsters union.

On February 25, 1994, Bufalino died of natural causes in a Pennsylvania nursing home at the age of 90.

Frank "The Irishman" Sheeran

Frank Sheeran Circa 1970
Photo courtesy of Charles Brandt

Charles Brandt's book recounts that Francis Joseph Sheeran was born to Thomas and Mary (nee Hansen) Sheeran in 1920. Growing up in the depression era, one of Frank's childhood memories was getting buckshot pellets removed from his backside by his mother after being caught stealing produce from a New Jersey farmer. Frank's father was Irish and a former amateur boxer. Whenever Frank got into trouble, his father threw Frank a pair of boxing gloves and used him as a punching bag. In ninth grade Frank was sent to the principal's office, and after being struck in the back of the head by the principal, Frank spun around and broke the man's jaw.

By age sixteen, Frank Sheeran was 6'1" 175 pounds thanks to his mother's Swedish ancestry. Raised Irish Catholic by their parents, Frank and his siblings lived in poor conditions. They moved frequently because of their father's inability to pay the rent. Frank joined a traveling carnival when he was seventeen, and a few years later, he joined the Army.

In December 1941, Frank was an MP at Lowery Field in Colorado. The day after Pearl Harbor, he was shipped to California for a Japanese invasion that never came. He signed up with the Army Airborne and deployed to the European theater where he was an infantry rifleman in the 45th Infantry Division, also known as the Thunderbird Division. With four hundred eleven days of combat experience, Frank Sheeran was molded into a cold-blooded killer. When Nazi troops were captured by his platoon, Frank had several occasions where he was ordered to kill the prisoners by superior officers. This would undoubtedly have been his introduction into the life of a hit man, teaching him to kill at the command of a superior.

In 1955, Frank found work as a truck driver. While in Endicott, New York, he met the man who would change his life forever. His rig was broken down at a truck stop when he was approached by a short Italian man named Russell Bufalino. The two men would become friends, meeting in Philadelphia for social occasions. Initially, Frank was unaware of Russell Bufalino's status as a high-ranking member of the mafia. In 1957, it was Frank Sheeran who dropped off Russell Bufalino at the infamous Apalachin meeting.

When Frank began doing "freelance work" for Philadelphia organized crime figures, he was brought before Russell and Philadelphia mob boss Angelo Bruno, where his life was almost cut short. The people Frank was working for were jeopardizing Bruno's business and there were going to be problems for people like that. Once Russell Bufalino vouched for Frank, his first ordered hit was to kill the man responsible for causing his reprimand with Angelo Bruno.

After that initial hit, Russell Bufalino would take Frank to new levels of corruption. He was sent to Detroit to help Teamsters President, Jimmy Hoffa with the problems he was having at the Local 299. Frank Sheeran was so good at making trouble "disappear" that he was lent to the Chicago Teamsters to handle their problems. He would later be given his own local in Delaware, where he would continue to work for Jimmy Hoffa and Russell Bufalino in whatever capacity they needed.

During Jimmy Hoffa's trials and tribulations, Frank Sheeran was such a common presence in the courtrooms that Robert Kennedy thought he was a member of Hoffa's family. He attended all of the hearings and visited Hoffa in Lewisburg Prison. It was Sheeran who delivered half a million dollars to John Mitchell, Attorney General to President Richard Nixon, to secure a pardon for Jimmy Hoffa in 1971. When Hoffa was released from jail, Sheeran was involved in his plans to regain control of the Teamsters. Hoffa warned Frank that if anything unnatural was to happen to him, that he had files that would blow the lid off many mafia secrets, including the involvement of organized crime with CIA plots to kill Castro and the assassination of President Kennedy.

Frank was extremely loyal to Hoffa, and he acted as the go-between for him and Russell Bufalino on large and small matters. In 1974 at an Appreciation Dinner for Frank Sheeran, Russell Bufalino told Frank to give Jimmy Hoffa a message, warning him not to rock the boat when it came to the union leadership. Frank's loyalty to Hoffa, however, would be tested a year later on a July afternoon in 1975. In September of the same year, Frank had to appear in Federal Court in Detroit to answer questions regarding the whereabouts of Jimmy Hoffa. Frank Sheeran chose to plead the Fifth.

In 1976, his name would be on a list of nine suspects believed to have been involved in the disappearance of Jimmy Hoffa. In 1979 Frank's lawyer, F. Emmett Fitzpatrick, sent *Hoffa Wars* author, Dan Moldea, a letter denying any role in the disappearance of Hoffa. He also requested a retraction and apology from Mr. Moldea for his allegations that Sheeran was involved. Steven Brill, author of *The Teamsters* was also contacted by Sheeran's lawyer and sued for defamation of character. Brill's defense team had the case dismissed on the grounds that Sheeran's reputation as a hit man was bolstered by the claim, and that the Federal government had been calling him a contract killer for years.

Several years later, Sheeran went to prison for labor racketeering and while in prison, Frank shared with a fellow prisoner, John Zeitts, many tales of his involvement in organized crime. Frank told John that on July 30, 1975 he drove to a house in Detroit where Jimmy Hoffa was already dead. His job was to drive the body to the Central States Sanitation Incinerator in Hamtramck, Michigan, where it was destroyed. Frank knew if this false information were to leak to Federal officials, he would have been indicted. Intrigued by the stories, Zeitts convinced Frank to write a memoir, so to speak, of his life. After telling Zeitts this well-known cover story about the Hamtramck Incinerator; Sheeran was feeding bits and pieces of the actual details to former Chief Deputy Attorney General for the State of Delaware, author, and lawyer, Charles Brandt. Finally, after Charles signed on as one of his lawyers, he secured Frank's release from prison on a medical waiver. Frank first began meeting with Charles in 1991 and in February 2002, they travelled to Michigan where Frank identified a house on Beaverland Street in northwest Detroit as the scene of Jimmy Hoffa's murder. He admitted to Charles Brandt that he was the person who killed Hoffa in the front vestibule of the house. Shortly after confirming his role in the murder of Jimmy Hoffa, he refused to eat and asked for a priest.

On December 14, 2003 at the age of 83, Frank Sheeran passed away in a nursing home in Pennsylvania.

Anthony "Tony Pro" Provenzano

A member of the Genovese Crime Family, Tony Provenzano was a vicious mafia captain. Like so many others in organized crime, he was placed into the Teamsters organization as a vice president for Teamsters Local 560 in Union City, New Jersey. A long time Hoffa supporter, the two became bitter enemies while serving time at Lewisburg Penitentiary. Provenzano wanted Hoffa's help in securing his Teamster's pension once he was released, but Hoffa refused and according to several published accounts told him "it was because of people like you that I'm in trouble in the first place". That statement and threats to kick mobsters out of the union if he was to become the president again, may have cost Jimmy Hoffa his life.

After Hoffa was released from prison, he was adamant in his quest to regain control of the Teamsters. He had appointed Frank Fitzsimmons, who he thought was his loyal lackey, to be his successor until he was able to get out of prison. What Hoffa did not count on was Fitzsimmons' involvement with Tony Provenzano to pay a large sum of money to President Richard Nixon, to place a condition in the pardon that Hoffa "does not engage in direct or indirect management of any labor organization until March of 1980." That slap in the face would cause Hoffa to begin his campaign to regain the Presidency of the Teamsters, and would set in motion the events that would come to a head in the spring and into the late summer of 1975. Provenzano knew how much of a hothead Hoffa was, and that he had an even bigger mouth. All it would take to place Hoffa on his bad side was for him to make a peep about kicking gangsters out of the Teamsters and give information to the Feds regarding the pension fund scams and Las Vegas. Hoffa was not just making a peep; he was on the rooftops screaming it at the top of his lungs. Provenzano would make his case to his old boss and Hoffa benefactor Russell Bufalino, and under the guise of having a sit down to work things out with Jimmy; he was behind the scenes planning Hoffa's murder. Sending his own mob soldier Salvatore "Sally Bugs" Briguglio and allegedly the brothers Steve and Thomas Andretta to Detroit for their part of the plan, Provenzano made himself an alibi at his Union City New Jersey Union hall on the day of Hoffa's disappearance.

However, Provenzano would be indicted on June 24 1976, for a murder that he had ordered back in 1961, of another Teamster official, Anthony Castellito. Tony Pro had Castellito killed because the man had run against him in an election. Provenzano saw Castellito as a threat to his power and ordered his murder. He told the men responsible for the hit to make the man disappear without a trace.

On June 21, 1978, Provenzano was convicted for the murder of Castellito and in 1988; he died in prison of a heart attack at the age of 71.

Anthony "Tony Jack" Giacalone

Anthony Joseph Giacalone was born in Detroit to Giacamo and Antoinette Giacalone on January 19, 1919. As the oldest of the seven children, Anthony would spend the day helping his father sell fruits and vegetables on Detroit's northeast side. As he grew older, Anthony would ally himself with like-minded criminals who would strive to become men of wealth and power. He became a member of the Detroit chapter of Cosa Nostra, also known as the Detroit Outfit or The Partnership. Allied with the Zerilli and Tocco families, Anthony and his brother Vito "Billy Jack" Giacalone were the Motor City's own wiseguys. In the 1950's Giacalone's power grew and his influence widespread as he and his brother Vito played important roles in the gambling operations conducted on behalf of the Outfit in Detroit, Michigan and Toledo, Ohio. He was caught on tape attempting to bribe Detroit Police Officer Sergeant Jim Thomas and later on was overheard bragging that he had the case dismissed by Judge Joseph Gillis Sr., with a payment of $10,000. Jimmy Hoffa was allegedly behind the payoff to the judge on Giacalone's behalf.

Although many thought Hoffa and Giacalone were close friends, the two put up with one another simply for business purposes. Giacalone was the middleman for Hoffa and the Detroit Outfit. Giacalone was supposed to meet with Jimmy Hoffa and Anthony "Tony Pro" Provenzano at the Machus Red Fox in Bloomfield Township, Michigan on July 30 1975 to help the two come to terms with their ongoing problems. While Hoffa was waiting for the men to show up, the usually elusive Giacalone made himself highly visible at the Southfield Athletic Club. The meeting never took place and it was his son Joseph's car that was borrowed by Charles "Chuckie" O'Brien to pick up Hoffa from the restaurant parking lot. Tony Giacalone was forced to appear in Federal Court following the disappearance of Jimmy Hoffa and many involved in the case believed he was being used as the fall guy for the missing ex-Teamster's apparent murder. When no case could be made from the evidence in the Hoffa disappearance, the IRS began a tax fraud case against him. First, a charge of fraud was aimed at Giacalone for his dealings with a Teamster medical coverage plan.

The deal struck in 1971 was to pay Tony Giacalone a fee for each member who was admitted to any of twenty Detroit area medical clinics and hospitals for treatment. The deal fell through when the story hit the papers but remained enough of a factor for prosecutors to use the deal to bring a case.

After a high profile trial Giacalone was found guilty and in 1976 sentenced to serve a ten-year term in a federal prison. Local authorities also won a second conviction against Giacalone for loan sharking when he allowed one of his family members to use his name to collect on an outstanding gambling debt. This offense earned Tony a twelve-year state sentence, which he was allowed to serve concurrently with his federal term. Tony entered the federal prison system in January of 1979, making a stop at the Lewisburg Prison before being sent down to a small federal prison in Alabama.

Giacalone spent three years in the Alabama prison before requesting that he be allowed to transfer to the federal prison in Milan, Michigan. Anthony Giacalone died on February 23, 2001 at the age of 82.

Salvatore "Sally Bugs" Briguglio

©Corbis

Briguglio was one of the FBI's prime suspects regarding the disappearance of

Jimmy Hoffa. He was a member of the Anthony Provenzano crew and operated primarily out of New Jersey.

Like his boss, Briguglio was also a Teamster official and was a Teamsters Local 560 trustee in 1972. After a short stay in prison for counterfeiting, Briguglio resumed his duties as a business agent for the New Jersey Local. Supposedly, his Teamsters job was a front for his other activities, as "Sally Bugs" was a hit man who killed at the orders of Tony Pro.

According to government sources, on July 30 1975, Briguglio was sent to Detroit to act as a front for Provenzano, who was supposed to have a sit down with Jimmy Hoffa and Detroit's Tony Giacalone. Allegedly, he and fellow Provenzano crew members Steve and Thomas Andretta were sent to wait at a house in northwest Detroit where Briguglio was supposed to be picked up by Charles "Chuckie" O'Brien and drive with him to the Machus Red Fox. When Frank Sheeran arrived at the house, Briguglio was in the front room window looking out a curtain, looking for O'Brien's car. There were two brothers from Tony Provenzano's crew in the rear of the house waiting in the kitchen. Chuckie O'Brien arrived and Sal left the brothers in the house, got into the back seat of the four-door

Mercury Brougham behind Chuckie with Frank Sheeran riding in the front.

They drove to the parking lot of the Red Fox where they found a furious Jimmy Hoffa. Jimmy was angry at being stood up for the meeting he was supposed to attend with Anthony Giacalone and Tony Provenzano, until Sally Bugs pointed out to Jimmy that his ally Frank Sheeran was in the car. Once Hoffa saw Sheeran, he got into the back seat next to Briguglio and the four men drove approximately thirteen minutes to 17841 Beaverland Street, in Detroit. Jimmy Hoffa and Frank Sheeran got out of the car and went up to the house and went in. Sally Bugs got into the front passenger seat and by the time Chuckie O'Brien had driven down the street, Jimmy Hoffa was lying on the floor of the house on Beaverland, having been shot twice in the head at close range.

Sheeran stated that Russell Bufalino told him that Chuckie O'Brien dropped off Sal Briguglio at the Central States Sanitation facility in Hamtramck, Michigan where he met up with the owner Pete Vitale, an old Purple Gang member. He was picked up later that afternoon by the Andretta brothers and left town from a nearby airport.

Like his boss Tony Pro and the Andretta brothers, Sal Briguglio would be forced to appear at the Federal Building in Detroit to answer questions regarding Jimmy Hoffa's disappearance. He would claim, as would his associates, that he was playing cards at the Teamsters Local in Union City New Jersey.

The heat was turned on Sally Bugs for several years by the FBI and he was approached by investigative reporters Steven Brill and Dan Moldea. Unfortunately, for Sally Bugs, instead of telling the two men no comment and keeping his mouth shut like Thomas Andretta, he was giving them information. He did not confess outright to anything but provided bits of information, and was most likely one of the leaks of false information regarding the Hamtramck Incinerator being used to destroy Hoffa's body. He was one of two people that could put Frank Sheeran in the car the day of the Hoffa disappearance.

Loose lips sink ships and on March 21, 1978, Salvatore "Sally Bugs" Briguglio was gunned down on Mulberry Street in New York City's Little Italy at the age of 48. Two assassins shot him multiple times in the head and chest. No one was arrested for the slaying. Frank Sheeran confessed to the hit to Charles Brandt and admitted that he and John "The Redhead" Francis were the shooters.

Thomas and Stephen Andretta

© Corbis

The Andretta brothers were reputed mafia soldiers under Anthony Provenzano from New Jersey. Police records and court documents show the Andrettas involved in criminal activity even in their teens. In 1967 Thomas was indicted in Middlesex County, New Jersey for loan sharking and in 1973 plead guilty to the charge. While awaiting that trial he was indicted with Provenzano henchman

Salvatore Briguglio in a counterfeiting ring. He was sentenced to fourteen months in prison.

On July 30 1975, he and his brother Stephen were supposed to be playing cards at their Teamsters Local in New Jersey along with Sal Briguglio and Tony Provenzano. Their alibi fell apart when eyewitnesses observed Sal Briguglio in Detroit, in the parking lot of the Machus Red Fox and later at the Hamtramck Incinerator. Frank Sheeran confessed that there were two brothers connected to Tony Provenzano, in the house on Beaverland Street in Detroit, waiting for Jimmy Hoffa to arrive. Frank was told by Russell Bufalino the disposal of Hoffa's body was coordinated by the Detroit people and that a funeral parlor helped by having the body cremated at a crematorium.

In August of 1975 the two brothers would be brought to Detroit to face Grand Jury hearings and Thomas Andretta refused to answer questions and plead the fifth. He was placed in Milan Prison for refusal to testify.

Steve Andretta was granted immunity from prosecution, which would not allow him to invoke the Fifth Amendment, but did not give any concrete answers that would help the investigation into Hoffa's whereabouts.

Thomas Andretta resides in Las Vegas, Nevada and his brother Steve passed away a few years ago.

Charles "Chuckie" O'Brien

Known as Jimmy Hoffa's foster son, Chuckie O'Brien was a part of the Hoffa family for years. His mother Sylvia Paris was a close friend of Josephine Hoffa and allegedly the mistress of Anthony Giacalone. In 1974 Chuckie and Hoffa had a falling out over Hoffa's problems with Fitzsimmon's leadership of the Teamsters. Chuckie was very close to the Giacalone family and on July 30 1975 borrowed Joseph Giacalone's car to run errands for Teamster Bobby Holmes. One of the errands was to deliver a fish to Bobby's wife in Farmington. O'Brien's account to the FBI for his travels that day, changed so many times that the FBI concluded that O'Brien was lying and was a dupe used by Anthony Giacalone to draw Jimmy Hoffa into a car with someone he knew. When Hoffa's son James P. confronted O'Brien regarding his father's whereabouts, O'Brien told the young Hoffa that he was acting "like a prosecutor".

The FBI's investigation into the disappearance of Jimmy Hoffa concluded that Hoffa was with Chuckie O'Brien and that O'Brien was a pathological liar and was not telling the truth about Hoffa getting into the car with him on that day.

Frank Sheeran would later explain Chuckie O'Brien's role that day and actually said that O'Brien did not know that Jimmy was going to be killed.

O'Brien was confronted by the FBI, in September 2001 with the fact that a hair from Jimmy Hoffa was found in the backseat of Joseph Giacalone's car. O'Brien scoffed at the discovery and said that since he was around Hoffa all of the time, that Jimmy's hair could have transferred onto him at any time and that was how the hair ended up in the car. After that visit from the FBI, O'Brien travelled to see Frank Sheeran at a bar somewhere near the Philadelphia airport, to tell Frank that he was not worried. However, O'Brien must have been concerned that certain folks like Sheeran would get the wrong impression believing he was cooperating with the FBI and tell them the truth about who was in the car with him on that July day.

O'Brien would make an appearance on the Maury Povich show to take a lie detector test to prove once and for all that Jimmy Hoffa was not in the car with him on July 30 1975. Chuckie passed the test.

O'Brien presently resides in Boca Raton, Florida, is in his seventies, and continues to deny that Hoffa was ever with him on that fateful day even though Frank Sheeran and several other witnesses have gone on record stating otherwise. The FBI and all of the Hoffa Strike Team members agree that Mr. O'Brien continues to hide the truth.

The Machus Red Fox

Machus Red Fox, Photo Courtesy of Andiamo's

One of the most famous restaurants in the world, but not because of its cuisine, chef, or owner. For over thirty years it has been known as the last place Jimmy Hoffa was seen alive. Presently called Andiamo's, this fine dining establishment in Bloomfield Township at Telegraph and Maple roads still serves as a meeting place for the affluent in Metropolitan Detroit.

Hoffa was not dressed properly for a meeting there, his golf style shirt and slacks would not have allowed him to dine there or even get past the coat check girl to use the rest room. In dressing like this, it was apparent to the FBI agents who investigated Hoffa's disappearance that he knew the meeting he was supposed to attend was not going to be in the restaurant, that it was a halfway point to a more private setting.

Eyewitnesses observed Hoffa using the pay phone at the adjacent Damman's Hardware front doors. A short time later, he was observed getting into a car occupied by three other men. The car drove off onto Telegraph Road, southbound to an unknown destination and Jimmy Hoffa was never seen again. That destination remained a mystery until one of the occupants of that car finally told the truth about the last ride of Jimmy Hoffa to Charles Brandt. The man's name was Frank Sheeran. It is interesting to note that the restaurant's basement would become the Strike Force headquarters for the FBI in the weeks after Hoffa's disappearance.

17841 Beaverland Street
Detroit, Michigan

Photo courtesy of Rick Wilson

Homeowner Rick Wilson knew there was something peculiar about his two-story, half brick bungalow, he just could not pin point it. When he purchased the home in 1986 from its second owners, he made some repairs, removed a kitchen door and gave the outside wooden trim an overdue paint job. Strange things were happening at the house, nothing you could put a finger on, but something just felt odd about the house to the Wilson family.

Rick, being a religious man would not speak of anything supernatural, but he admitted something about the house made the hairs on his neck stand up on several occasions.

In 2004, he was home and heard a knock on the door. A man was standing on the front porch and asked to speak to the homeowner. Behind him, standing on the sidewalk was a television cameraman. Rick let the men in and Fox News Channel reporter Eric Shawn asked him if he could ask some questions about the house. Eric Shawn advised Rick that there was a strong possibility that a murder of a very famous person had happened in Rick's home. Rick looked at Eric Shawn and the cameraman and said, sardonically, "You mean like Jimmy Hoffa?" The cameraman turned as pale as a ghost and Eric Shawn nodded in amazement.

It was explained to Rick that in fact, a man named Frank Sheeran claimed that he killed Jimmy Hoffa in the house and that the body was cremated. Rick said the house once had its own trash burner and that it used to be located in the basement.

Long before Rick Wilson or the family before him lived in the house on the tree-lined Beaverland Street of Northwest Detroit, the home was owned by a retired Detroit Public School teacher who also worked as an executive secretary for the owner of Montgomery Ward Department stores. She used the house during the school year, but in the summer time would reside in suburban Detroit. During the summer, she would rent out rooms to boarders at the Beaverland house and the summer of 1975 was no different from any other. Neighbors would recall that she did not spend much time at the house, and in 1975, there was an older gentleman renting a room there. No one ever paid him any mind, but folks would remember that he would stroll up to Grand River Avenue and used a walking cane to do so. He seemed to be quite elusive and none of the neighbors remembers ever speaking to him. One of the neighbors even suggested that he seemed to be an old mafia guy, but that was just a thought.

Family members of the retired schoolteacher, (who had passed away before the 2004 investigation) were questioned by Charles Brandt about the house being equipped with its own trash burner. One of the questions asked was would it have been large enough to incinerate a human body?

It was explained that although the trash burner did get hot enough for burning refuse, it was not designed to burn large objects and that a body would have to be in pieces to fit inside of it. It would have taken several hours, if not days to burn human remains and the trash burner would never get hot enough to cremate bones.

In 2001 a white vehicle turned the corner of Curtis Street at Beaverland and stopped in front of the house. Rick Wilson's son remembered seeing the vehicle and told his father that their house was being watched. Rick did not know it then, but he had just been paid a visit by a man who had been to his house before.

On July 30 1975, Frank 'The Irishman" Sheeran had entered the house with Jimmy Hoffa, for the purpose of killing the former Teamster's boss. In 2001, he returned with his lawyer and biographer Charles Brandt on a confession/pilgrimage. He had to come clean for what he had done to his friend Jimmy. He gave the directions to Charles and they drove Telegraph Road to Seven Mile, turning onto Berg Street, then south to Curtis, passing the Rogell Golf Course and onto Beaverland. Approximately a thirteen minute drive from the Machus Red Fox. Charles notified Eric Shawn at Fox News Channel and shortly after Frank passed away in a Pennsylvania nursing home, the story broke in late May 2004. The location of the murder scene of Jimmy Hoffa had finally been found. Charles Brandt had written a book about Frank Sheeran's life and his confession of the Hoffa murder in the book, *I Heard You Paint Houses*.

The media circus that unfolded next was tremendous. Experts from around the country, retired FBI officials, State, and local police gave their opinions and most agreed that the Hoffa disappearance had been solved. Fox News Channel received permission from Rick Wilson to examine the floorboards of the house for blood remnants, and hired a forensics team to come and spray luminol on the suspected area of the crime scene. After they received a positive hit for blood on the floor, they notified the FBI, who in turn contacted Oakland County Prosecutor David Gorcyca to give him a heads up of what they had found. Bloomfield Township Detectives were dispatched to the scene as well as Michigan State Police forensics teams. Luminol was sprayed at least two more times, and then the floorboards were taken up and shipped to the FBI crime lab for DNA testing.

After a few weeks, the media frenzy died down, but gawkers and the curious public (this author being guilty of this as well) would drive by and look at the house.

In February 2005, the FBI announced that the DNA from the blood taken from the floorboards was not Hoffa's. Life went back to normal for Rick Wilson and family and interest in the house subsided. At least for a while.

Everybody has a Theory

Over the course of the past thirty years, I have heard just about all of the theories relating to the disappearance of Jimmy Hoffa. I am certain that even if I were to list all of the ones I have heard, from either reading about them in the newspaper, or various news broadcasts, there would be new ones that would pop up from those who claim to know somebody that knows somebody who heard that Hoffa was (fill in the blank)

You can imagine, as I have been working on this for over three years now, whenever the topic would be brought up, even after Frank Sheeran's confession is explained at length, that folks would still tell me what they think happened to Hoffa.

One story I will share is from 1993, when I had no idea or ever dreamed that I would be involved with this case. In the summer of 1993, I was two years into my enlistment in the Marine Corps. For most of that summer I was hanging out with my friend and fellow Marine, Mike Knoll.

Mike was from San Diego and we would head down to his folks house and spend the weekends there and frequented the downtown district. We were both interested in Law

Enforcement and one night we happened to be walking by a Bail Bonds office. We thought it would be a kick to go into a "real bounty hunters office" and ask if there were any bad hombres we could go hunt for the guy. The Bail Bondsman introduced us to one of his skip tracers, and I am not joking the dude looked like Dwayne Chapman, also known to Television viewers as Dog the Bounty Hunter. Anyway, Mike and I introduce ourselves and I tell the Bounty Hunter that I'm from Detroit. He says, "You're from *Dee-troit*, the land of Jimmy Hoffa."

I smiled and said, "Yeah, my Grandpa is a Teamster." The next thing out of the Bounty Hunter's mouth is, and I am not making this up; "You know the San Diego Mob was behind Hoffa's disappearance." Like I said, everybody has a theory.

The prevailing theories are as follows, and believe me; each one can have a life of its own in the court of public opinion. These are the top theories I have heard over the years.

1. Hoffa was kidnapped and while driving to a house near the Machus Red Fox, had a heart attack and died. He was ground up into pieces and shipped to the Florida Everglades.

2. Hoffa was kidnapped and held at gunpoint, hit over the head and strangled in the car, died, and was taken to Roland McMaster's Horse Farm in Milford, Michigan and buried next to a barn.

3. He was killed and put into a drum of lye, oil, cement, etc. and shipped to New Jersey according to Donald "Tony the Greek" Frankos and buried in the end zone of Giants Stadium in East Rutherford.

4. He is in the cement footings of the Mackinac Bridge.

5. He is part of the cement overpass at the Southfield Freeway/Jeffries Freeway (I-96) in Detroit.

6. He was crushed in a car compactor somewhere in Detroit.

7. He was killed and then taken into the basement of the Machus Red Fox and chopped up. (My aunt Janette DeCourcy told me that one)

8. Hoffa was placed in the cement foundation of the Renaissance Center (General Motors HQ) in Detroit. (It was under construction at the time)

9. He was incinerated at the Central States Sanitation Incinerator in Hamtramck, Michigan.

Last on the list, because like I said, there are several hundred variations, this one is the most ludicrous I have ever heard:

10. Hoffa was given memory fogging drugs and put in a safe house for several months and when the time was right was forced a stow away on the Edmund Fitzgerald, which as we all know sank on November 10, 1975 and is at the bottom of Lake Superior.

These are just a sample of the theories that the public and media have been spewing at parties, restaurants, on television shows, in major motion pictures and around the water cooler. I was embarrassed and refused to watch any more coverage of the Milford Horse Farm dig in May of 2006 when the local news media thought it would be cute to air a story about the people in Milford selling "Hoffa cupcakes" on the side of the road.

Can one imagine the outrage if folks in Boulder, Colorado would have made JonBenet Ramsey freezer pops or Columbine cookies and tried to sell them? It might seem different because those cases involve children, but still folks tend to forget that Mr. Hoffa has a family that has suffered for more than three decades.

Grand Lawn Cemetery
Detroit, Michigan

During the first week of September 2001, a news broadcast reported that the FBI found a hair belonging to Jimmy Hoffa in a car that his foster son, Charles "Chuckie" O'Brien, was driving on July 30 1975. DNA confirmed that Hoffa had been in the car. Mr. O'Brien continued to deny that Hoffa was ever in the 1975 four door Mercury Brougham and brushed the news off as another ridiculous attempt by the FBI to place Hoffa with him that summer afternoon. After the Hoffa story aired, it was pushed to the wayside by the tragedies of September 11.

In late May 2004, *The Fox News Channel* announced a break in the case. A house in northwest Detroit was given as the location where Jimmy Hoffa was murdered, per a deathbed confession given by Frank "The Irishman" Sheeran, a Teamster official and friend of Hoffa's. I must admit that I had never heard of Frank Sheeran before that newscast. I watched the reports closely, and when a Detroit Television station gave the location of the house, the wheels in my head started turning. Frank Sheeran, to my knowledge, was the first person to give detailed information regarding the pick up of Hoffa from the parking lot of the Machus Red Fox, and the route to the house where Jimmy Hoffa was murdered. When it was announced that the house where Hoffa was killed on the 17000 block of Beaverland, I jumped out of my seat. The house was only a mile away from the neighborhood where I grew up.

When I was a Detroit Police Officer, I worked at the Eighth Precinct and patrolled the neighborhood where the house is located. I knew that one way in to the neighborhood was from Grand River Avenue. When the story broke, I surmised that the drive from the Machus Red Fox would have been from Maple to southbound Telegraph then onto Grand River and up to Beaverland Street.

Being very familiar with the area, I thought to myself, "I wonder what Hoffa was thinking as they passed by Grand Lawn Cemetery." I watched the *Fox News* reports of floorboards being taken from the Beaverland house and checked for DNA. An independent company hired by Fox News Channel sprayed luminol on the floorboards. Luminol is the "glow-in the dark" liquid that helps investigators find traces or evidence of blood at crime scenes. Their luminol tests showed a positive reaction for blood from the front vestibule all the way into the kitchen area. The hired forensics team was excited by their discovery, as it corroborated Frank Sheeran's claim that Hoffa was killed in the house. The story was plastered all over the airwaves and internet before the book *I Heard You Paint Houses* by Charles Brandt was released. A short time later I went to Borders Books and read the last chapter of the book.

Frank Sheeran's account of the drive to the house was chilling. When I read that they had picked up Hoffa at the Machus Red Fox and travelled south on Telegraph road, turned left onto Seven Mile, drove east and made a right, I knew exactly where Sheeran was talking about. The drive he described was from Seven Mile to Berg Street, then past the

Rogell Golf Course, left at Curtis and up to Beaverland.

It made perfect sense. Not only did Frank Sheeran give the exact location, he described the only other way you could drive to that neighborhood from Telegraph Road. His depiction of the ride, the murder, and intimate knowledge of the floor plan of the Beaverland street residence was convincing. I bought the hardcover of the book shortly after and read it cover-to-cover, obviously focusing on the last few chapters. I was convinced that Frank Sheeran was telling the truth that he was the man who killed Jimmy Hoffa by shooting him twice in the head, and that it happened at 17841 Beaverland Street in Detroit, Michigan. A few months later, I even took a drive past the house and got chills up my spine. Here it was one of the biggest mysteries of the past thirty years and part of it took place not a mile from my old neighborhood.

On February 14, 2005, which coincidentally is Jimmy Hoffa's birthday, it was announced by the FBI that the blood tested from the floorboards did not match Hoffa's DNA. Only one article ran by the Oakland Press in May of 2004 explained that every time luminol is used, DNA is destroyed.

A colleague of mine, Detective Maureen Brinker, gave me some insight into luminol. She explained that there are several formulations of luminol and although no commonly used formulas "destroy" DNA, if too much luminol is used, the DNA can be "washed away" or diluted. There are certain formulas that protect DNA better than others. It is also known to luminesce on itself, meaning if too much is used, it can give a false positive for blood remnants. False positives can be obtained from certain metallic items such as pennies, which are used at the lab as a positive control. Certain cleaners, most commonly bleach and biological substances that contain plant peroxidases can also create false positives.

However, when all of the talking heads announced the blood was not Hoffa's, no other explanation was given. There was no mention that the thirty-year-old evidence had been deficient in the first place, it was just simply stated that the blood was not Hoffa's. I found out later that a four-year-old boy had lived in the house in the 1980's and had an accident in the vestibule of the house, and his DNA was found. The other collected evidence came back as inconclusive.

Charles Brandt's book explained that Frank Sheeran remembered a piece of linoleum was placed in the vestibule and hallway area, to catch any blood left by Hoffa's gunshot wounds to his head.

Once it was announced the blood was not Hoffa's, the media dropped the story. In the court of public opinion, this alone almost debunked Frank Sheeran's account. It seemed as if the public's interest in the Beaverland house vanished.

Unlike the folks that hang on every word that is fed to them by the media, I did not doubt for one moment the validity of the house on Beaverland, or Frank Sheeran's confession. He knew too many details about that house. He knew what it looked like inside and knew key information about the kitchen area and hallway that no one just driving by could guess. He knew it was a borrowed house and that the owners or the people staying there would not be home when Jimmy Hoffa walked through the door. How would he have known this, much less remembered almost thirty years later unless he actually been inside of that house?

I asked myself, "If I were to get rid of a body from that house, where would I take it?" One day I was talking to my Grandfather and told him my thoughts about Hoffa's last ride. I explained to him how I was mistaken about the way Hoffa had been driven to the

Beaverland House. I realized my thought about "I wonder what Hoffa was thinking when they passed by Grand Lawn", was a mistake. It was like a brick came out of nowhere and hit me in the head.

I began to piece together my theory. *Houses* quoted Frank Sheeran as saying that Hoffa was cremated and that a funeral home friendly to the mafia was involved. There it was right in front of me. The house where Hoffa was murdered is only a few blocks away from Grand Lawn Cemetery.

Another option close by was the Northrop and Son's Funeral Parlor just down the street on Grand River Avenue and Northrop street. How easy it would be to have the body driven over to one of those places and simply destroyed. I shared my theory with a few close family members, thinking that someone involved in the investigation, like the FBI, Fox News or even Charles Brandt, would have looked into these places. A year went by and it seemed nothing else was going to be brought up about the Beaverland House.

Then, on the 30th anniversary of Hoffa's disappearance, David Ashenfelter of the Detroit Free Press wrote a story that time-lined Hoffa's life and his sudden disappearance on July 30 1975.

In that article retired FBI Agent Robert Garrity was asked what he thought happened to Hoffa's body. He stated, "They probably drove a short distance and disposed of it. I've always thought that they incinerated it or put it through a car crusher."

I read the article and decided to e-mail my theory to Mr. Ashenfelter. This is the actual e-mail sent to him:

Mr. Ashenfelter,
I am currently a Police Officer in (suburban Detroit). I grew up about a mile away from the Beaverland/Curtis House where Frank Sheeran supposedly killed Mr. Hoffa. I read the book by Charles Brandt and believe it is the most accurate account of the Hoffa disappearance and murder. At your convenience, I would like to speak to you about your article from Saturday's paper. It's regarding the Grand Lawn Cemetery and the Former Northrop & Sons Funeral Home. If I am not mistaken, both of those places had access to Cremation Services.
They are just across Grand River from the Beaverland House. If this is old news, please let me know.
Jeff Hansen 07/31/05

The next day Dave Ashenfelter responded to my email. When we spoke later in the afternoon, I explained my theory and asked if he knew if anyone else had brought up the funeral home or the cemetery before. He had never heard of any connections between these places and Hoffa's disappearance. He asked where they were in relation to the Beaverland House, to which I replied, "Right across Grand River Avenue". He stated that my theory was one of the best he had heard, but it would be very hard to prove. After talking for a while longer, he suggested that I call the FBI agent in charge of the Hoffa file at the Detroit FBI Office. On his advice, I spoke to an FBI agent (I do not recall his name) identifying myself as a police officer, and explained my theory to him. It was only two days after Ashenfelter's story ran, so everyone and their brother was calling in tips. I did not want to be lumped in with a bunch of Hoffa fanatics. I thought my theory would have more credibility coming from a fellow law enforcement officer.

I asked the FBI agent if what I was telling him was old news, and if anyone had looked into the Northrop and Sons funeral home or Grand Lawn Cemetery. He had not heard of those two places either and thanked me for my information. Because I am a police officer, and knowing that this FBI agent may want to confirm who I was, I notified my Internal Affairs supervisor Commander Don Helvey.

I shared my theory with Commander Helvey and advised him that I had notified the FBI. He agreed that my theory made the most sense. In the past, we had several conversations about the mafia in general, and he had always been interested in the Hoffa disappearance.

Almost a year passed with nothing about Hoffa in the news until a man named Richard "Iceman" Kuklinski came forward with a confession of his own. He claimed to have kidnapped Hoffa and killed him, sending parts of his body all over the United States and even to Japan. In my opinion, it was just another crackpot's attempt at fifteen minutes of fame. (Mr. Kuklinski's statements about Hoffa and other high profile cases were debunked by Law Enforcement a short time later.) This "story" piqued my interest again, so I attempted to contact Charles Brandt. Unable to get in touch with him, I left it alone for a month or so, and that is when the big announcement came. The FBI had a witness that gave the location of Jimmy Hoffa's body. A prisoner named Donavan Wells was giving them information they had already looked into back in 1976. Back then, Wells was a boarder at a horse farm in Milford, Michigan owned by former Hoffa associate and Teamsters official Roland McMasters. Wells claimed that he had observed a rug being buried near a barn on the property on July 30, 1975 and that Roland McMaster nudged him, smiled, and said, "There goes Jimmy". His claims struck me as highly suspect, and garbage is all the FBI found under the barn. I was amazed, however, at the FBI's eagerness to believe a man who was seeking a deal for his conviction regarding the sale and transport of large amounts of marijuana.

The story was pushed upon the FBI by Wells' attorney who threatened to go to the press if they did not go to the farm and check for Hoffa's body.

In fact, Hoffa investigator Dan Moldea believes that Wells was telling the truth and that it was the folks that worked for McMaster that were responsible for the murder and disposal of Hoffa's body. The problem with that entire Roland McMasters theory for me was that not one eyewitness ever puts any of McMasters "henchmen" in the Giacalone car driven by Chuckie O'Brien, and everyone (except for Frank Sheeran) that comes forward with "new" information is attempting to get their jail sentence reduced.

After the first week of the now infamous dig, I e-mailed Ashenfelter, again, this time asking his opinion on the story. He was guarded, but gave the Horse farm story 50/50. After the dig did not turn up any remains, not even a horse's neck bone, I reminded Ashenfelter that I felt very strongly about the Northrop Funeral Home and Grand Lawn Cemetery, and that I wished to share my information with Charles Brandt. Ashenfelter responded that he had forwarded my e-mail to Charlie, and if he were interested, Charlie would contact me. Two weeks went by and I heard nothing.

That all changed on Wednesday May 31 2006.

Just to satisfy my own curiosity, I drove to Grand Lawn Cemetery and asked a few questions. It was about 2:00 pm when I went into the front office. I spoke to a few of the office staff and told them I was doing research for a book about local cemeteries. I explained that I grew up in the area and that as a teenager I used to ride my bike through the cemetery almost on a daily basis. I asked if cremations were performed at the cemetery, and if so, were any performed back in the 1970's? They were not sure about back then, but they knew cremations were not performed at the cemetery anymore. I thanked them and went on my way. I drove around to the grounds keeper's garage and looked inside to see if there were any cremation ovens, which are also known as *retorts*. I saw one of the grounds crew nearby and asked if the garage was the location where cremations were performed.

He told me cremations were done up at the front, in the mausoleum, but the cremation ovens did not exist there anymore. I drove up to the mausoleum and noted a placard on the wall stating the building was dedicated in 1973. I then drove down Grand River to the old Northrop and Sons Funeral Home. I spoke to the current owner Mr. Ellis and asked him if there had been cremations performed at his funeral home. He advised me that there were no cremation ovens in his building and that he did not believe that there would have been cremations performed at any funeral home back in the 1970's.

At that point, my focus shifted solely to Grand Lawn. I was driving back home when my cellular phone rang. It was my wife, Heather, and she had some very interesting news. Charles Brandt had just called our house and he wanted me to give him a call.

Once I had Charles on the phone, I told him my background and that I had read his book, believing that Frank Sheeran's confession was the truth. I explained just how close the house was to Grand Lawn Cemetery and that I had just left the cemetery where I was told cremations had been done there, but I needed to go back to get more information. He was excited, to say the least, so I e-mailed him an aerial photomap, showing the cemetery in relation to the Beaverland house. He was amazed. We went over what I should be looking for at the cemetery, he hoped I could locate a smoke stack or chimney on the building, "that would be great," he said.

The next day, June 1, 2006, I was unable to get to Grand Lawn until the afternoon. When I arrived, I asked if I could get into the mausoleum building, into the room where the cremations were performed. I was told the building was locked up but that I would be able to get in the room the following day. I drove to the mausoleum and again noticed the placard on the building showing that it was dedicated in 1973 and that it was called the Holden Chapel. The area I was hoping to get into was a service area in the middle of the building.

If my theory was correct, I was going to see the very room where Jimmy Hoffa may have been cremated. I was prepared to walk into an empty room and hope to get a picture of a chimney or ductwork leading to the roof. I took the day off work, which was June 2 2006. I had it set up with my friend Marty Sigarto to meet me at the cemetery to drive my van while I videotaped the drive from the Beaverland house to Grand Lawn Cemetery's mausoleum.

Once Marty showed up, I asked the Grand Lawn staff if the mausoleum doors could be opened. I was told it would be opened for us in a few minutes. That gave us time to drive up to Seven Mile and Berg street. I began videotaping from the corner of Seven Mile and Berg and then southbound on Berg to Curtis street. We came around the corner and I continued to videotape the rear and then the front of the Beaverland house. We paused there, and I gave a short synopsis of the historical nature of the home and then we proceeded to drive south on Beaverland and up to Grand River Avenue. We drove west up to the front entrance of Grand Lawn and then proceeded down a road that led to the mausoleum's service drive. I got out of the van still videotaping as the service doors of the Holden Chapel were opened.

I was expecting to walk into an empty room and was very surprised as I walked through the doors and found that two cremation ovens were still there. It was at that point for me, that my "hard to prove theory" became very interesting.

Note: *The lack of cremation facilities at funeral homes was also confirmed by 35-year veteran Mortician Monty Wulff, of the Charles R. Step Funeral Home in Redford, Michigan.*

Now, the ovens/retorts were not proof but just the fact that the scene of the murder was only two minutes away from the crematorium and that everything that Frank Sheeran told Charles Brandt fit with this theory of mine.

Sheeran told Charles Brandt that the body was disposed of within an hour of the murder. According to Sheeran, the two brothers from New Jersey took Hoffa's body and it was cremated within an hour of his death. For me, Grand Lawn became the number one place to dispose of Jimmy Hoffa's body. I reported what I had discovered immediately to Charles Brandt and sent him a copy of my videotape. I can only say that Charlie was very happy with my discovery. However, the discovery of the cremation ovens just opened up more questions for us to answer.

Over the month of June and into July 2006, I was going back and forth to Grand Lawn in hopes of finding the cremation logs. It was July 26 on one of my several trips to

Grand Lawn that I found logbook number 13, dated June 4, 1975 to April 28, 1978. I flipped to the page with that infamous date of July 30, 1975. This was an interment logbook.

*Names have been changed at the request of the family.

The logbook shows that on July 30 1975 a Cora Jackson* was interred at her husband's gravesite. Mr. Jackson had died several years prior. In the space provided for her date of death, it was left blank. Her cause of death was listed as "Not Stated". Next to her information she was listed as a cremation. Looking at this logbook entry, one could easily assume that Cora Jackson was cremated at Grand Lawn. In the logbook, there was a space provided for next of kin information. I was able to contact the Jackson family and spoke to Cora Jackson's daughter. I asked her if her mother was cremated at Grand Lawn before she was interred with Mr. Jackson.

The daughter stated that her mother had died in Florida in the beginning of July 1975 and that she was cremated in Florida.

The family arranged with Grand Lawn Cemetery in mid July, to have the grave of Mr. Jackson prepared for the interment of Mrs. Jackson's cremains. The family had the cremains shipped to them and they called

Grand Lawn a week prior to have their father's grave opened to have her mother's urn placed on top of the casket. The cremains were taken to Grand Lawn by a family member and dropped off at Grand Lawn and turned over to the office. The family was not present when the cremains were interred in Mr. Jackson's grave on July 30 1975. The family had a small service a few days later.

The daughter's account of her mother's service did not match up with the logbook. Nowhere in the Grand Lawn logbook does it state that Mrs. Jackson was cremated in Florida. The dots were connecting. Frank Sheeran had told Charles Brandt that *everything was going to be a straight shot, everything close to everything else.* This cemetery is two minutes away from the house on Beaverland, and not only did this particular cemetery appear to have a crematorium, on the specific date of Hoffa's disappearance, a woman was listed in that cemetery's logbooks as a cremation, but she was cremated out of state several weeks prior.

My thoughts turned to the possibility that the Jackson grave could possibly have two urns. After a few weeks, it was verified that only one urn was in the grave with the casket of Mr. Jackson.

It was important to eliminate the possibility of the cremated remains of Jimmy Hoffa being put into an open grave on that day. It could have been that his ashes were simply dumped in the trash, scattered into the wind or taken out to the small man-made pond that is next to the mausoleum/crematory. Later on in the investigation, I found out that another more logical and easier explanation was waiting for me.

While finding the logbook was extremely important, one vital lead presented itself.
I discovered the name of the former director of the cemetery, Bob Baker.

He was in charge of Grand Lawn in 1975. Using the internet I tracked him down and gave the information to Charles Brandt who decided that it would be best to speak to Mr. Baker in person. For the next several months I gathered as much information as I could and would travel to Grand Lawn at least twice a week to look for more documents, especially anything relating to the mausoleum and crematorium.

On September 8 2006, Charles Brandt arrived in Detroit to have a look at what I had uncovered. I picked him up from the airport and we immediately made our way to Grand Lawn Cemetery. Once we arrived there, we were given access to the logbook and to the mausoleum/cremation facility. After going over the logbook and touring the room were the cremation ovens are housed, we drove to the home of Bob Baker. According to his neighbors, he and his wife were out of town. Charles gave the neighbor his business card and a copy of *I Heard You Paint Houses* and asked that he pass them along to the Bakers' when they got back into town. With a forty-five minute drive back home and no other information to gather, Charlie and I decided to call it a night.

It was September 9 2006 when Charles Brandt and I went back to Grand Lawn and had another look at the cremation ovens. We also went into the main office building and checked the record books that I had found in July. We also found a cremation logbook that began in 1979 and ended in 1997, but could not find its counterpart that would have been used with the interment log dated June 1975 to April 1978.

In the afternoon, we drove to the Beaverland street house and met with the homeowner Rick Wilson. Charles was on a first name basis with Rick, and when we showed up, Rick was surprised, but happy to see the man who helped make his home a historical landmark. I had driven past that house on numerous occasions, one of them being to time the drive from the house to the cremation room at Grand Lawn. It was on this day, that I was given access to the house where Jimmy Hoffa was murdered. Charles and I met Mr. Wilson out in front of the home and he graciously led us on a tour. Charles had been in the house a few years prior to this, but this was my first time. When I walked into that doorway and looked around, I was spellbound. I cannot explain it by writing it, it is just one of those feelings you get when you know you have walked into history. The front door vestibule is tiny; two people walking through it at the same time would be quite difficult. I walked in first with Charles behind me. My first glance was down the narrow hallway that led to the kitchen area and then to my right.

The front curtains were drawn and the large front room led to a dining room. The house was quiet; Rick was the only one home that day, so it was as though I was observing what Jimmy Hoffa saw as he walked into the house. I went to turn around and Charles was there. Rick had gone towards the kitchen and was standing in the hallway where the floorboards had been removed two years prior. Charles stepped to my left and I took a close look at the door, to see how thick it was. In my mind, I wondered that if two gunshots went off in that doorway, was the door thick enough to muffle the sound? After examining the door, there was no doubt in my mind that the door was thick enough to muffle just about anything. It was the original door to the house and was the door that Jimmy Hoffa would have tried to open, as he figured out that no one was there to meet with him. As I went to turn the doorknob to open that heavy wooden door, I felt a pointed finger put to the right side of my head from behind. Charlie stated, "That my friend is how quickly it happened."

Rick showed us the rest of the house and I examined the areas where the floorboards were removed. The investigators that had them removed were gracious enough to repair Rick's home after they tore it up. Charles and I spoke to Rick for about thirty minutes in the house, where we explained to him what we thought happened to the body of Mr. Hoffa. We invited him to take a ride with us and we all drove over in my van to the mausoleum. We spent another half an hour there and then drove Rick back to his house.

On September 10, Charles took my wife Heather and I to dinner, at what used to be the Machus Red Fox. It is called Andiamo's now but the building exterior and famous overhang still looks close to what it looked like back in 1975. We had a fabulous dinner and we spoke about Charles' recollections of Frank Sheeran and the original investigation of how and when they found the house where Hoffa was killed. When we left, Charles pointed out the area of the parking lot where Frank Sheeran told him where he and the others in the Giacalone car had picked up Hoffa. Charles also pointed out the hardware store where Hoffa had used a payphone to call his wife to let her know he had been stood up.

Charles Brandt and author Jeff Hansen in front of Machus Red Fox (Andiamo's) September 2006

On September 11 we went to Grand Lawn to speak with the groundskeepers to gain more insight into the cremation procedures and their recollections of former employees that may have worked at the cemetery back in 1975. Charles and I spent the day looking over more paperwork and going over the plan when we would catch up to Former Director of Grand Lawn, Bob Baker.

On September 12, we made our way to the Baker's residence. We walked up to the home and knocked on the door and Mrs. Baker answered it. A very nice lady, she politely asked us what we needed and Charles explained to her that he had dropped off his business card and book with the neighbor for her husband to look at. She recognized Charles from the book and let us both in without hesitation. Mrs. Baker said that she and her husband had looked over the book and remembered hearing the story about the house and Jimmy Hoffa on the news a few years prior. Charles and I were led to the family room where Mr. Baker was sitting. For the few months after finding Bob Baker's name in the records at Grand Lawn, I had wondered if there was a possibility of his involvement. I had expected that Charles Brandt and I would be turned away at the door, obviously bringing up events that no one would want to admit being a part of. However, when we sat down with the Bakers and they began answering questions without blinking an eye, I was put at ease. They explained the cemetery business to us and confirmed that the Holden Chapel Mausoleum was built in the early seventies and that Grand Lawn was performing cremations on a daily basis.

Charles continued to ask questions like a true professional. It was a learning experience to say the least. The Bakers explained to us just how easy the process was for cremations at any cemetery if a funeral home were to provide the proper paperwork, called a Burial Transit Permit. Filled out with the deceased's name and date of death, the paperwork would be signed by a funeral director and would be given to the persons who would be picking the body up to deliver it to the crematorium.

The process went like this: The funeral home would pick up the deceased person from their home, hospital, or morgue. Sometimes the funeral home would have a body pick up service working for them that employed various folks to drop the
body off with the paperwork and a fee of $110.00 dollars. The body would sometimes be brought in a cardboard box with a plywood bottom and that the box was never opened to verify if a man or woman were in the box or even if there were more then one person in the box, no one would know. The box would be put in the oven (retort) and a switch would be

flicked and the body would be turned to a pile of coarse asphalt like substance after a few hours. The Bakers were asked how many people had access to the cremation room, and Bob Baker answered that he was the main person with the keys to the entire cemetery and that he would give his employees access on a case-by-case basis, when needed.

The question arose if there was a possibility of a cremation happening without his knowledge, after hours, and he said that was highly unlikely. Charles also asked the Bakers if there would be any reason for a logbook to be missing. Mr. Baker and his wife said there should not be anything missing from the cemetery office that everything was kept in an upstairs vault in the side office of the main building. It became very clear to me and Charles Brandt that whatever funeral home helped with disposal of the body, the way Frank Sheeran explained, that they simply assisted by giving the persons tasked with cleaning up the house and body a falsified burial transit permit, cremation box and possibly an unmarked funeral home vehicle. We spent over an hour speaking to the Bakers and to say we left the house excited is an understatement.

It had been a long three months since I had decided to start digging so to speak, around

Grand Lawn, and two years since I first thought about the cemetery being involved. To have the dots connecting the Beaverland House to Grand Lawn was a big deal for me. However, my excitement would only last about a week and a half. Charles left Detroit and went home to Idaho. With this new information, he was convinced that Grand Lawn Cemetery was the last piece in the puzzle of the Jimmy Hoffa case, that it all made the most sense because of its close proximity to the murder scene.

A week or so later, I received a call from Charlie, that he had more information from the Bakers, that during a follow-up phone call, Mrs. Baker recalled that Jimmy Hoffa's mother Viola was buried at Grand Lawn! What a surprise that was and I drove to Grand Lawn shortly after that revelation and asked the office personnel to look up Viola Hoffa in the records. Sure enough, she was buried there and died August 28 1975, almost a month to the day her son disappeared.

The interment card showed that her brother Steve Riddle paid for the plot. What a coincidence. There was nothing sinister going on but still, a strange coincidence nonetheless. Some more information was given to Charles by the Bakers in that follow up phone call.

Mrs. Baker told Charles that old burial transit permits were kept in the basement in another vault and the missing logbook could be there. When Charles flew back to Detroit in late September, I met him at the airport and we drove out to Grand Lawn and scoured the office basement for the missing logbook and the old burial transit permits. We found some old transit permits, but none for the year 1975, and no 1975 cremation logbook. We did find the cremation logbook for 1979, and were allowed to *borrow* it for our next meeting with the Bakers.

I remember the day very well because it was my birthday, and Charles received a phone call from his friend, retired FBI Agent Joe Pistone, aka Donnie Brasco.

While we were sifting through the old basement vault, Charlie had to speak to Joe about their then upcoming book, *Unfinished Business*. Charles told Joe to wish me a happy birthday and handed me his cell phone. That would be the highlight of my day because when we arrived at the Baker's residence to discuss the information they had provided, and with the logbook from 1979 in hand, we went over the entries in the book that began with entry number one. After going over the information in that logbook, the Bakers were now uncertain if the cremation ovens were in the building in 1975. When Mr. Baker said, "You guys, I think you have the wrong cemetery" I was surprised. The Bakers explained that the retorts were installed several years after the building was constructed and that other cemeteries in the area, like Evergreen on the east side or Woodmere in southwest Detroit, had crematoriums for sure. Charles and I drove back to Grand Lawn and went to the office one last time and saw the staff there.

When we were about to leave we drove past the mausoleum and I told Charles, "Look, at those doors there, they are way to short to be shoving those ovens into that room, after the building was constructed, and what about the year the place was built, look at the placard on the wall. Remember, it says it was dedicated in 1973." As I said that, Charles was taking pictures of the service doors to the cremation room.

I walked over to the placard. I am certain I yelled a string of swear words I will not repeat here. I called for Charles to come over to the door of the Holden Chapel and stood there pointing at the brick wall like one would point out a dead body. Charles walked up to me and asked what was wrong. I pointed at the brick wall where the Holden Chapel placard *used to be*. It had been ripped off the wall. The only things left on the wall were holes where the placard had been attached by screws. Charles and I went to the office and asked the staff if anyone knew when the placard had been stolen. We were told that it had been discovered missing and reported to the Detroit Police around a week prior. That put the theft somewhere around the second week of September, right around the time Charles and I were asking questions about the cemetery.

Could it have been vandals that ripped the placard off the wall for scrap? After all, it was made out of some sort of metal and cemeteries all over Detroit were being hit left and right for their copper and brass fixtures. That very well could be the case. However, that placard had been on that building for over thirty years. It is a very strange coincidence that it just happened to be stolen during the exact same time that Charles and I were asking questions about the very building the placard had been attached to. However, we were not working on your everyday run of the mill murder investigation either. I drove Charles back to the airport and we said our goodbyes. He went back to Idaho, and I drove home.

When I arrived home, my wife and kids had a cake waiting for me. After celebrating my birthday, they could tell I was not as happy as I should be, and my wife asked me what was wrong. I explained to her what the Bakers had said and that the placard on the building was gone.

This sign was stolen September 2006.
Photo taken by author June 2006.

As I spoke to her about it, it dawned on me just how important the pictures and video I took of the cemetery, mausoleum, and placard were. When I went back to work I told Commander Helvey that the Bakers were not sure if the cremation ovens were at Grand Lawn in 1975.

Over the next few weeks after Charles flew back to Idaho, I spent some time attempting to find out when the Mausoleum was built, so that I could track down the specific date of construction and correlate that event with the cremation retorts being installed closely thereafter. I called the State of Michigan, Wayne County and the City of Detroit buildings and permit departments. They all had the same answer for me. Cemeteries in the State of Michigan are exempt from pulling permits. They do not have to show plans, or have anyone come out to inspect the buildings.

After my initial investigation at Grand Lawn, I decided to look at the next closest cemetery with a crematorium in relation to the Beaverland house.

Evergreen Cemetery
Detroit, Michigan

My information gathering would take me to Evergreen Cemetery on the eastside of Detroit on Woodward Avenue between Seven and Eight Mile. A privately owned cemetery that sits next to the much larger Woodlawn Cemetery, I discovered that Evergreen has *three cremation ovens* that have been in use since 1942 and two of them were used on July 30 1975. The records show two females were cremated that day. (Woodlawn also had a cremation oven in 1975, but logbooks show no cremation for July 30 1975.)

Evergreen Cemetery is a fifteen-minute drive east on Seven Mile, then a left turn onto Woodward Avenue and approximately a half mile south of Eight Mile.

If the men tasked with disposal of the body had a burial transit permit, and cardboard cremains box, and an unmarked funeral home station wagon, they could have driven Hoffa's body to any cemetery or crematorium in Metro Detroit, right? The answer is sure, they could have. However, they most definitely would want to go to one that had been used before by the funeral parlor associated with the Detroit Outfit, via Pete Vitale. Mr. Vitale was the owner of the Hamtramck (Central States) incinerator, where Sal Briguglio was dropped off to meet back up with the brothers from New Jersey who worked for Tony Provenzano. He was a key person of interest in the Hoffa disappearance and was observed at the same meeting a week after in New York, where mob boss Fat Tony Salerno was debriefed about the Hoffa hit and disposal of the body. According to sources close to the case, Mr. Vitale's name was brought up as the person who had direct connection to the funeral home that helped with getting the body to the crematorium.

It was interesting to find out that Evergreen had cremations that day, and thinking back to what Frank Sheeran told Charles Brandt as documented in *I Heard You Paint Houses*, *"The house was just a few miles from where Jimmy's remains would go. Everything was going to be very close to everything else, all of it was a straight shoot. You most definitely couldn't go driving around any kind of distance and making lots of turns with Jimmy's body in a car. Who in their right mind would transport such a high profile package a block longer than was necessary".* I believe Frank Sheeran was attempting to give more clues with that statement. One must think of the capability and knowledge that the Detroit Outfit had for this type of work. Whoever it was that ordered the murder of Hoffa planned it down to the minute. With schedules to keep, alibis to consider, they are not going to screw around with having even the remote possibility of getting into a car crash, pulled over by a nosey traffic cop or struck by a bolt of lighting. Whoever was tasked with this did not want any extracurricular activity going on during this coordinated effort.

So, I called Charles and told him about Evergreen Cemetery and explained the interesting facts I found there and how it was a straight shoot from Beaverland.

Charles advised me to dive back in and keep looking for information, paperwork or someone that would prove if Grand Lawn had cremation ovens in 1975 or not and that Evergreen was definitely a place of interest.

The Media

In November 2006, Charles Brandt was contacted by *KLAS TV* Las Vegas Channel 8, whose investigative reporter George Knapp was airing a three part program about the Hoffa disappearance. During the last night of the series, Charles planted the flag about the cremation ovens at Grand Lawn, making it official information regarding the Hoffa case. George Knapp's focus was on Thomas Andretta, one of only two people still alive that were implicated in the disappearance of Jimmy Hoffa. Since Thomas Andretta lived and worked in Las Vegas, naturally KLAS TV wanted to show the trail of the Hoffa Mystery led there.

It was a fantastic synopsis of the case and it was a great feeling to see a picture of the cremation oven on television.

In July 2007, I was contacted by *Detroit Free Press* writer Joel Thurtell. City Clerk Mary Ann Rilley introduced me to him, in 2005 when I was promoting my crime novel *Warpath*. Joel was interested in self-publishing and wanted to write a story about how I was able to do it. He wrote for a community style magazine published by the

Free Press that was dedicated to special interest stories like Detroit area parks, glassblowing and canoe trips down the Rouge River and interviewed me about my book. It was a great article and it helped my sales tremendously. So, Joel calls me and asks what my next project is going to be. I told him I was working on a sequel to *Warpath* called *Target: Somalia*, but that it was on the backburner because I was busy working on a game adaption of *Warpath* with Kevin Siembieda of Palladium Books. He thought that was interesting and I asked him if he had looked at my website. He said, yes, that it was looking very good. I told him he should look at the Hoffa page I had created. He said "Jimmy Hoffa?" I ended up explaining the whole story to him.

Joel was extremely interested and we met for lunch at Scotty Simpson's Fish and Chips in Detroit and spoke about the Hoffa case.

After lunch, we drove to the Beaverland House and then we drove over to the cremation room. I went into detail about everything that Charles Brandt and I had uncovered and Joel wrote what would be the first article that explained the discoveries at Grand Lawn and Evergreen Cemetery to readers across metro Detroit.

Later in 2007 the E! Channel was in the middle of producing a show called "*The 20 Most Shocking Unsolved Crimes*". They had scoured the internet for information on the Jimmy Hoffa disappearance. They found Joel Thurtell's article about my discoveries at Grand Lawn and Evergreen Cemeteries. He was interviewed for an hour and they decided to cut what he said down to about thirty seconds. Charles Brandt was also contacted, not only for the Hoffa story, but also as a commentator on several other unsolved crimes. Charles told the world that only two minutes away, from the house on Beaverland Street, in the Grand Lawn Cemetery were a pair of cremation ovens. I have to say, when my friend Charlie said that on national television, my heart almost jumped out of my chest. What a feeling that was. I have the telecast saved on my DVR and still get a rush when I see it on TV. I called him as soon as I saw it and thanked him repeatedly.

So, as time went on, after it was all said and done, I went to work on my other writing projects and focused on my real job and family life. I had to let this case go for a while.

Not that I had lost interest, obviously not, but it was definitely time to take a break from it. For a guy who rarely ever visits the graves of his loved ones, going back and forth to

Grand Lawn and other cemeteries in Detroit was beginning to wear on me. I had proven my point as far as I could take it at the time. But, I soon learned that this case has a life all its own. I had my website, I got Grand Lawn (and even Evergreen Cemetery) on the map of public interest with the Joel Thurtell article, and I thought I was done with what I set out to do. It was around January of 2008 that I decided that I should use my case notes that I had kept since beginning my research at Grand Lawn, that I decided to outline this book. With my main priorities being my wife and four kids, an outline was all I had time to do, and I had other projects I was working on.

In May of 2008, I received a cryptic, ominous email from a man who claimed he knew that I was right about Evergreen Cemetery and where the cremains (the ashes) of Jimmy Hoffa were. Since my contact number is on my website, I received a voice message from this individual. I decided to email him back to see what it was he was talking about. He called me on my cell phone one day and sounded extremely scared, to the point of paranoia, and began stringing me along for over a week. I called Charles Brandt and told him about the email and the phone call and he told me that he had received an email from the same fellow.

Charles was correct in assuming that this man was not someone to take seriously, which I found out soon after for myself. I was lucky that I only had this one person attempting to give me false leads and cannot imagine the flood of calls Charles or the FBI received while they were conducting their interviews or investigations of the Hoffa case. After that learning experience, I went back to my other projects and normal everyday life for a while.

In October 2008, I received a phone call from Charles Brandt. He had just received confirmation that Martin Scorsese was going to direct the movie adaption of his book *I Heard You Paint Houses* and that Robert DeNiro was going to play Frank "The Irishman" Sheeran. All of that work and investigation on Charlie's part as it related to Frank Sheeran had finally paid off. A movie based on his book. That was some fantastic news. It was all over the internet and the days following the announcement, I noticed a huge surge on my website hit counter, simply because of the keywords I have attached to the Hoffa page. It was interesting to see how just the mention of a movie being made, especially by a high caliber director like Martin Scorsese can grab the publics attention and spike interest in this case once again.

In late February 2009, I looked at the outline I had created for this book. I figured it was time to begin writing memories down and start setting my own thoughts onto paper. I decided it would be best to contact Jimmy Hoffa's family and to let them know what I had found, before they heard about it on the news or happened to see this book on a shelf in Borders or Barnes and Noble.

I was able to contact Judge Barbara Crancer, Jimmy Hoffa's daughter and explained to her that I had some information to share with her. She was polite and asked me to mail my case notes to her and that she needed to read Charles Brandt's book again. I mailed her out the case notes and phoned Charles to let him know that she was going to read over his book again and look at my notes about Grand Lawn and Evergreen. Charles had sent both Barbara Crancer and James P. Hoffa original hardcover versions of HOUSES, back in 2004. In 2008 James P. Hoffa, now the President of the Teamsters was in Pennsylvania stumping for Presidential candidate Barak Obama when he was asked by the *Times Leader* reporter Jerry Lynott, if he had heard of the book by Charles Brandt and subsequently, the confession of Frank Sheeran. James P. stated that he had read the book, and claimed that Frank Sheeran was a strange character, and that anyone reading that book would have to believe that Frank Sheeran was a one-man crime spree, with all the murders he claimed to have been the killer.

Now, Charles had sent the Hoffa siblings the original 2004 version of the book.

James P. was obviously referring to Frank's claim that he was the triggerman behind the Crazy Joey Gallo hit in 1972. James P. would not have the follow up information that was in the updated version of HOUSES, released in 2005. That is the version that has the epilogue, where Charles Brandt explains that an eyewitness was discovered that happened to be in Umberto's Clam House on the night of the Gallo hit. That person identified Frank Sheeran as the lone shooter. So, James P. and his sister Barbara were basing their assumptions that HOUSES was just a tall tale of mob hits and mayhem concocted by Frank Sheeran to help establish money for his family when he passed away. What Jimmy Hoffa's children did not know was that not only was this eyewitness Charles Brandt discovered one hundred percent credible, the NYPD investigators who worked the case also knew the hit was the work of a lone gunman. I called Charles and he asked me to send Barbara Crancer the epilogue section of HOUSES, that way she could see that there was more to the story and that there was credible eyewitness corroboration of Frank Sheeran's account. I mailed the information out to Barbara and about a week later received a letter from her. She thanked me for my interest in the subject of her father's murder and that I had spent a great effort and time to verify Frank Sheeran's account of his involvement. Mrs. Crancer added that her family was not looking forward to a proposed film based on Sheeran's story and that thirty-four years have not eased the painful memories of their loss. She had received the information I had mailed and ended the letter asking me not to contact her again.

I called Charles Brandt and explained to him what Barbara Crancer had written in the letter. He was not surprised. For the Hoffa family to validate Frank Sheeran's account of their father's disappearance and murder, they would have to admit that all the misdeeds and criminal activity, even the murders that Frank Sheeran confessed to, would have implicated their father in those past sins. In HOUSES, Frank goes into explicit detail about the Teamsters Union and Jimmy Hoffa's involvement with organized crime. He also explains the utter hatred Jimmy Hoffa had for the Kennedys and an insider's viewpoint of the Hoffa mindset. Frank even gives an account of the possibility of Hoffa's knowledge and culpability in the assassination of President John F. Kennedy.

This information would not bode well for two extremely staunch Democrats, who have been working all these years to cleanse themselves of the past sins of their father. They do not want to lend one ounce or iota of credibility to Sheeran's claims for those reasons. Even though it was Barbara Crancer who wrote Frank Sheeran asking him to tell the truth about his involvement in her father's murder, the fact is she would have rather he admitted it without besmirching her father's name and dredging up the murky waters of the 1950's and 60's.

According to Steven Brill, author of The Teamsters, James P. Hoffa was well aware of his father's organized crime connections and even defended them. His excuse for the alliance was that it was Jimmy Hoffa's answer to big business' past use of thugs and criminals. Hoffa was only using them with the *end justifies the means* mentality and that he planned to kick them all to the curb once his power was re-established.

After contacting Barbara Crancer, I decided to place a phone call to Rick Wilson, owner of the Beaverland House hoping to set up a meeting with him to go over his recollections of the 2004 investigation. He remembered who I was and was interested in speaking to me about his house and Grand Lawn. We met in early March of 2009 and discussed the case and the timeline of the house and the surprise visit he received from Eric Shawn from *Fox News Channel*.

Return to Grand Lawn Cemetery

After that meeting with Rick Wilson, I dropped him off at his home and decided to drive to Grand Lawn. It had been over a year and a half since I had driven through it and I decided to walk around the mausoleum just to see if there was something I had missed on my previous visits. It was about three in the afternoon on a Saturday, and the place was deserted. It had been snowing most of the day and I was the only person around. I walked around the building looking for other markings or placards, but only found the empty space where the Holden Chapel placard used to be. I went to the back of the building, and noticed something that I should have noticed back in 2006. It was something that was so simple, that it should have been one of the first things I looked into after the Bakers told Charlie and I that they were not certain if the ovens were in the building in 1975.

Behind the mausoleum, near the man-made pond, are gas pipes coming out of the ground. If the building was constructed with gas lines, electric and water, there had to be a record somewhere of the date of service. On Monday morning, I placed a call to Michcon Gas Company and asked the service person if there was a record of gas service for the main office at Grand Lawn, which is 23501 Grand River Avenue. She stated that gas service to that address began in 1967. I asked her if there was record of another building just west of the main office. She told me that yes, there was another building on the grounds of the cemetery, and that its address was 23651 Grand River. I now had the actual address of the mausoleum. I asked when the gas was turned on for that specific building she said, 1979. The air was let out of the balloon again. However, I followed up that call with two more, one to Detroit Edison and one to the Detroit Water Department, both of which had no record of 23651 Grand River.

No record? I sat back for a while and thought about the fact that gas service did not begin at the mausoleum until 1979. I spoke to Charles Brandt about this and as we talked it out, the simple answer came a few minutes later.

Grand Lawn opened in 1908. On the register of deeds plot book from the City of Detroit, it shows ownership by *Grand Lawn Cemetery*. It did not change ownership to another company until 1986, when it became a part of the Woodlawn Cemetery Group. After that, it changed ownership more than seven times. The answers came to us both as I asked myself rhetorical questions. Questions like, "Grand Lawn's office had been there since the early 1920's. It did not have gas running to it until 1967? The mausoleum chapel placard stated that it was dedicated in 1973, meaning it had to be built in 1970-1973. So, from the time it was built until 1979, the building chapels had no heat, electricity, or running water? Charles said there was no way that could be possible. How much money would they lose in business if there were no services able to be held in the chapel area without heat, in the event of a winter service? That mausoleum, chapels, and cremation room were all built together for the purpose of having services whenever needed.

I went to the register of deeds and they had no record of any building on the grounds of Grand Lawn Cemetery, which was something I already knew. Remember, cemeteries in Michigan are exempt from permits. Charles also had another explanation for the gas service not showing up in records until 1979. When the building was constructed, they had gas ran to it, and it would be a simple task for a plumber to cut in a line to the building and have gas going to the building without anyone knowing it. It's a simple task for a professional plumber, or someone who knew what they were doing. I verified just how simple it is with a family friend who has worked in plumbing and he told me it would not be at all difficult to do, if you had equipment and the right tools.

Another explanation is simply this, every time ownership changes, the date for the utilities change, for example, the main office did not show that it had water until 1962, electricity until 1994. The inconsistencies in records also throw things off and can let the air out of a balloon very easily. However, I am a very persistent individual and I was not finished yet.

I decided that it would be best to question the former director at Grand Lawn, Bob Baker and his wife Janet again. I was able to catch the couple on the phone and Mrs. Baker remembered that I was the young man that had accompanied Charles Brandt to their home back in 2006.

I explained that some new questions had come up and that I believed that a Burial Transit Permit with a false name was used and that whoever it was at Grand Lawn that helped put the body into the cremation oven had no idea that Mr. Hoffa was in the cremation box.

She said, "Oh is that how you think it happened? That makes the most sense." I wanted to let her know that I was in the process of finally writing a book regarding the cemeteries and to go over some questions that I had regarding the construction of the mausoleum and chapels.

She told me that the following week would be fine for me to come to their house and interview her and Bob once again.

Another piece in the puzzle was that of a former Grand Lawn grounds keeper who I will call *John*. I originally knew about John back in 2006 but was never able to interview him to ask his recollections of Grand Lawn and the mausoleum. As my luck would have it, I found him in late February 2009 and only told him that I was doing research into the history of Grand Lawn Cemetery.

I did not tell him anything about the Hoffa case. I met with him for lunch on March 4 2009 and had a questionnaire for him to answer. He was very forthcoming with his answers (in italics on the following pages).

Questionnaire for Grand Lawn Cemetery

SUBJECT: "John"
March 4th 2009
Interview conducted by Jeff Hansen

What year did you begin working at Grand Lawn Cemetery?

I began working at Grand Lawn in 1989, but got into the cemetery business in 1977.

What year was the Mausoleum/Holden Chapel built?

In 1973 or 1974.

When it was constructed, was the building equipped with Gas/Electric and water?

Yes, it had everything.

How did you know this, since you did not start working there until 1989?

Whenever I would start working at a place, because my job was also maintenance I would check the buildings plans to see what was what, in case things broke down.

Were the cremation ovens in the building in 1973?

Yes. The building was built for that purpose, Mausoleum, two chapels with the cremation room in the middle.

Were they in use in 1975?

Yes.

How many employees had access to the cremation ovens?

Just about all of them.

What were their names?

Most of them are dead, now and I really don't remember.

What were the names of the attorneys/partners that owned Grand Lawn in 1975?

I'm not sure.

Were there any rumors or personal accounts that anyone at Grand Lawn was associated with Organized Crime? (The Detroit Partnership, The Outfit, La Cosa Nostra)
Not to my knowledge but I've always had thoughts about an incident.

What incident is that?

I think what it is we are talking about, James Hoffa?

When did you think that?

I had always thought that because the Machus Red Fox is just up the street from Grand Lawn when
the story a few years ago came out about that house in Redford, being where he was supposedly killed.

The House you are referring to is in Detroit, and its two minutes away from Grand Lawn. When did you start thinking about this?

Back in 1989, just because it would have been so easy to put Hoffa in one of those ovens and no one would have known it.

For the record, did I mention anything about Jimmy Hoffa to you at all before you answered that question?
No.

It was extremely interesting to find that other folks had thought about the possibility that Jimmy Hoffa was cremated at Grand Lawn, and that no one else had called the FBI or any other law enforcement agency with this theory. John also explained that it was not uncommon, either in the 1970's or today for groundskeepers, crematorium operators, or cemetery directors to accept kick backs or bribes from the public or contractors.

Later that afternoon, I met with Bob and Janet Baker at their home. Mrs. Baker welcomed me into the house and I sat down with her and Mr. Baker in the same room I had been in back in 2006. This time I didn't have my professional interrogator Charlie Brandt with me, but I had learned quite a bit from watching him work. I asked the Bakers if it was okay to record the session, because it would be easier for me to transcribe what they said later on when I went to write everything down. They had no hesitation whatsoever and before I began taping, I again told them both that I wanted them to rest assured, that I did not think they were intentionally involved with the cremation of Jimmy Hoffa, that I believed a faked Burial transit permit was used. The Bakers were happy with my statement and I began recording the interview. I used the questionnaire as a template, and began by asking Mr. Baker what year he began working at Grand Lawn.

The following are the excerpts of what would be over an hour of discussion of the Bakers recollections and especially regarding the construction of the mausoleum and installation of the cremation retorts.

BOB AND JANET BAKER INTERVIEW

Hansen: Mr. Baker, what year did you begin working at Grand Lawn Cemetery?

Bob Baker: 1958.

Hansen: Until when?

Bob Baker: Around 1988, nearly thirty years.

Hansen: Mrs. Baker you began working here?

Janet Baker: 1964 to 1969 or 1970, then a part time basis in 1982.

Hansen: When were the mausoleum/chapels built?

Bakers: Between 1969 and 1970

Hansen: And the building was dedicated in 1973 as the Holden and Burton chapels, with the Burton chapel being the one on the north side, correct?

Bakers: Yes.

Hansen: When the building was built, was it equipped with electric, gas and water?

Janet Baker: Oh, yes.

Hansen: Now, the cremation ovens, in the middle when were they installed?

Janet Baker: The cremation retorts, the one against the wall is a metal one, was put in 1970, 1971.

Hansen: And the second one went in?

Janet Baker: A few years after the first one, around 1979, a man and his son from Canada installed that one.

Hansen: Who installed the first one?

Bob Baker: That was from Anaheim, California. The second one was put in around eight years after the first one.

Hansen: So that first one was there, and being used in 1975?

Janet Baker: Oh, yes.

Hansen: How many employees had access to the cremation room?

Bob Baker: I used the men as they were needed, so there was never just one person with access.

Mrs. Baker: There were probably around nine.

Hansen: Who owned the cemetery in 1975?

Bakers: That was a group of attorneys. They had offices in Grosse Pointe.

Hansen: Were there any rumors that you heard of anyone at the cemetery being involved in Organized Crime?

Bakers: No, not at all, never.

Hansen: If a funeral home had a burial transit permit to bring a persons body to the cemetery in a cremation box, would you have any reason to look inside the box?

Bakers: No, there would be no reason to do that.

During the rest of the interview, the Bakers told me the names of former groundskeepers that worked for Mr. Baker at Grand Lawn and a few days later, I spoke to the two gentlemen separately on the phone. They were not aware of what I was contacting them for. The two recalled that Grand Lawn had at least one cremation oven in use in 1975 and that the process for cremation was as simple as having a burial transit permit and flipping a switch. When I was finished speaking to them, I checked my picture files and found that
I had indeed taken a photo of the first oven. All this time, since finding the two ovens at Grand Lawn, it was the second one that was installed in 1979 that was getting all the attention. It was the one that was opened on my original video and the one I had my picture taken in front of by Joel Thurtell.

The first oven next to the wall, which does look different from its partner, according to the Bakers and their former employees was at the facility in 1975. To have that recollection by five different sources was very important to say the least. The Bakers and the groundskeepers also gave me information that I did not have previously. They explained to me that inside of the Holden Chapel, on the walls are name plaques also called niches, and that inside of the niches are cremains boxes. Above the smaller niches are large storage bins and inside of the bins are unclaimed cremains.

Back in 2006, I had noticed a cremains box with a name and date on it left in the cremation oven/retort room. It was from 1987. I had always wondered what was done with cremains that were not picked up by the funeral home or the deceased's family.

My question had been answered and my travels would take me back to Grand Lawn in April of 2009. I was placed in contact with the head groundskeeper who set up a day for me to have the larger unmarked bins/niches opened to see what was inside.

On May 8 2009, accompanied by my friend Marty Sigarto, I was given access to the Chapel. One of the groundskeepers assisted myself and Marty and opened every large bin, all sixteen of them and we found cremains boxes dated in the 1980's. Nothing was found with the date July 30 1975. I had hoped to find a cremains box with that date on it, with a false name but I was not surprised that it was not in those large bins. However, the groundskeeper and office manager told me that the smaller niches, which were unmarked, were unable to be opened, because they are possibly owned by someone, and may have cremains in them. I would have to find the owners and request permission from each one of them (there are over twenty) to get the niches opened. They also advised me that they had no idea where the logbook was for those niches, that they had no way of finding who owned them.

Grand Lawn Cemetery Cremation Oven/Retort

Interior of Holden Chapel. Large squares in top of photo are storage bins that are used to hold unclaimed cremains. Opened cremains niche containing cremains box from 1980

During the last few weeks of writing this book, I spoke to Mrs. Baker again and went over her recollections regarding the chapels and cremation retorts. The 1979 logbook was brought up once more. Mrs. Baker stated that she was not one-hundred percent certain that the first cremation oven was inside of the mausoleum in 1975 that she wanted to take a trip out to Grand Lawn to see the 1979 logbook for herself. That particular logbook, to Mrs. Baker's recollection was the first logbook and in her opinion, it meant that Grand Lawn was not performing cremations in 1975. Several questions needed answering. Was there an oven placed in the building shortly after the mausoleum was constructed? Was there a reason it was not used for six years? Is it possible that the 1979 logbook goes with the cremation oven built in 1979 that the logbook from 1975 is missing?

These questions went unanswered until June 16 2009. I met with the Bakers at Grand Lawn and Mrs. Baker handed me some documents from the All Furnace Corporation of Anaheim, California. The paperwork, which was faxed to Mrs. Baker gives the date that the first cremation retort was installed in April of 1979.

DIGGING FOR THE TRUTH

Finally, after three years I was able to eliminate Grand Lawn as a key place of interest in this case. Some may still have questions as to the recollections and statements made by the other groundskeepers and the Bakers for that matter. The facts are that documentation always trumps memory in this type of investigation. Thirty-four years have passed and memories from that period in time are fading and it was extremely important to have the documents surface that the Bakers provided. They were also the reason I began focusing on Evergreen Cemetery in 2006. All of that work at Grand Lawn and the interviews with the Bakers and the former groundskeepers would prepare me for the events that would happen next.

All Roads Lead to Evergreen

Opened in 1905, Evergreen Cemetery has been privately owned and operated by nearly the same family for decades. The mausoleum, erected in the 1920's, houses three cremation retorts. The retorts have been in use since 1942. They are still operational and in use today. According to the present manager, all three cremation retorts can be run simultaneously. It takes approximately four hours to cremate a body.

Also, in the attic of the mausoleum is a storage space where over two-thousand unclaimed cremains boxes have been kept since 1950.

On July 30 1975 there were two females cremated at Evergreen. This cemetery and its crematorium have been used in the past by the Bagnasco Funeral Parlor, which was mentioned by Frank Sheeran in his confessions to Charles Brandt. In fact, a source in the funeral business confided to me that when he would go to deliver a body to Evergreen for cremation, it was commonplace to find bodies (in caskets or cremation boxes) lined up out the door waiting to go into the cremation ovens. There would be no one around to take the body and if he really wanted to, he could have started the ovens by himself and no one would have been the wiser. This was commonplace in the 1970's.

Evergreen Mausoleum

Evergreen Crematorium access door

Evergreen Crematorium retorts

To have a better understanding, I returned to Evergreen in June 2009 and was able to go into the cremation room. This cemetery is less then ten minutes away from the Hamtramck Incinerator, and an additional ten minutes to get to Detroit's City Airport on Gratiot. This would have been a round trip for the men tasked with the disposal of Hoffa's body. Evergreen Cemetery fits with everything Frank Sheeran confessed to Charles Brandt and how the two brothers from New Jersey left town after meeting back up with Sal Briguglio at the Hamtramck Incinerator. What is also extremely important to understand is how simple and easy it was to have a body cremated back in 1975. As I was finishing this book, more information came to light. I met with the president in charge of Evergreen Cemetery, Ole Lynklip, interviewed him about the cemetery's history, and focused on the 1970's. We spoke about the cremation retorts and the procedures for accepting a body for cremation at his facility. I explained to him my reasons for asking those questions.

When the topic turned to Jimmy Hoffa being cremated at Evergreen, Mr. Lynklip smiled. He was skeptical at first but after explaining the information I had found, he agreed that it was possible. If fake paperwork was given to him or his employees, or if a body was brought in a wooden casket or cardboard cremains box, there would be no reason to look inside of the box.

The paperwork was the key. It is also important to note that Hoffa, at the time of his disappearance, was only five foot six, one hundred and sixty-five pounds. The burial transit permits I have for the two women cremated that day show that they were eighty and ninety-four years old. I am certain at that age, either of the two women could have easily shared space in their caskets, or cremains boxes with Mr. Hoffa if that was the way the deed went down. It has been extremely difficult for me to track down their next of kin. Is it possible that one of these women did not really exist, that a fictitious name was created for a falsified burial transit permit?

More information would come from that interview with Mr. Lynklip and it was in the form of the name of the man in charge of Evergreen back in 1975. His name is Arthur Stickles and I found his number in the phone book and called him. I started out the conversation the same way I had with all of the others; I asked about the history of the cemetery. Mr. Stickles was very helpful and had a keen memory of the cemetery he had worked in for many years. After a few minutes of going over the background of Evergreen, I asked Mr. Stickles a list of names that were associated with organized crime in Detroit. Like Mr. Lynklip, he did not know any of those folks personally, but had heard their names mentioned in the newspapers. When I asked him about Jimmy Hoffa, there was a pause. He told me that he remembered that after Mr. Hoffa's disappearance that he was paid a visit by two men that he surmised were Law Enforcement, possibly FBI agents. They asked him if he had any *unusual* cremations on or about July 30 1975. Mr. Stickles told them that he had not, that he had nothing out of the ordinary occur during that timeframe. The two men took him at his word, and left without asking to see the logbooks or burial transit permits!

All this time I had hoped someone back then asked the questions I've been asking for the past three years, but to find out that they never asked to see the logbooks is amazing to me to say the least.

Mr. Stickles and I went over the time line of when Hoffa was picked up at the Machus Red Fox, to his murder on Beaverland and then the possible drive to Evergreen. Mr. Stickles said that if a casket containing a body would have arrived at his crematorium in the late afternoon that it would have waited until the next day to be cremated because the cemetery would have had the issue of dealing with overtime. It is an approximate assumption that Hoffa was dead by 3:00 pm, the house cleaned and his body put into a body bag, taken to the car, and then driven to Evergreen fifteen minutes away. That puts the body arriving at the crematory at approximately 3:45 pm. Quitting time was 4:00 pm at Evergreen, but the problem with that is that the two brothers who worked for Tony Provenzano had to get back to New Jersey that evening. (Remember they had alibis to worry about)

Is it possible that they would have left the body of Jimmy Hoffa waiting in a crematory overnight, even if he was in a casket with some other person? That is highly unlikely.

Frank Sheeran was told that everything was finished within an hour of Hoffa's murder.

The men tasked with the disposal of the body would have made sure that it was in the cremation retort. I asked Mr. Stickles if he believed it could be possible that the body of Jimmy Hoffa was cremated at Evergreen. He said he believed it was possible.

This is a man, along with Mr. Lynklip, who had spent his entire life dedicated to Evergreen. To admit to the possibility of his cemetery being involved in this plot speaks volumes. He also made sure that I understood that the folks that worked there were a very tight knit group and that he could not imagine anyone there being involved in helping gangsters get rid of a body on purpose.

I believe the deed was done right under everyone's noses, and appeared to be as legitimate as not to raise the suspicions of businessmen like Mr. Lynklip and Mr. Stickles or the folks that worked for them.

One of the last phone calls I would make before this book went to press was to the Bagnasco Funeral Home. I spoke to Mr. Bill Bagnasco, whose great-grandfather had started the family business at the turn of the century in Detroit.

Knowing that Frank Sheeran had already linked his family name to the Hoffa case in Charles Brandt's book, I kept my questions vague.

I started by asking where the original Bagnasco Funeral Home was located, in 1975. He said that the family had moved the business to St. Clair Shores in 1964, but that one of the original Bagnasco funeral homes was located at East Grand Boulevard at Vernor, and that they kept the one on Vernor open for a few years even after moving to the suburbs. I asked if the Detroit location was still open and used in 1975 and he said that it was. When asked what cemetery would have been used for cremations by his funeral home, he stated that Evergreen was used but back in the 1970's cremation was not as common as it is today. The location of the original Bagnasco Funeral home opened up more questions and more cemeteries for me to look at. During a follow up phone call, I decided to explain to Mr. Bagnasco where I had heard of his funeral home and that my questions were related to the Jimmy Hoffa case. I expected to be hung up on, but Mr. Bagnasco was professional and explained that he had never heard of Charles Brandt's book. He was extremely skeptical about any funeral parlor, much less his family's, being involved in helping dispose of a body by having it cremated, or providing the paperwork to do so. He explained several people would have to be involved and that someone at the cemetery would have noticed two sets of bones in the cremation retorts. He also said that for something like this to occur, that someone at the cemetery would have had to be involved.

He believed the whole thing to be a waste of time and that he was tired of his family's name being linked to every mafia story brought up by the media. He wished me luck and we ended our conversation. The statement he made about the two sets of bones being left over, (If Hoffa was put inside of the same box with someone else) is inconsistent with the statements made by every crematorium operator I have spoke to these past three years. What is left after cremation is a very coarse, ash-like substance, in a pile that is in the shape of the body. Sometimes bones are left, like the hipbones, and those are ground up by the crematory operator.

I can understand Mr. Bagnasco's feelings regarding his family's one hundred year old business and that he does not want to have any link to organized crime. After all, Frank Sheeran only mentions once in HOUSES that he heard that it was Bagnasco Funeral Home that was involved. There is no way to prove that. It is important to understand that this is part of the mystery surrounding this case that no one really knows what funeral home, if any, helped with this crime. I also found several other cemeteries that were located close to Detroit's City Airport, the most plausible escape route for Sal Briguglio and the two brothers from New Jersey. I found that Forest Lawn Cemetery is right next to City Airport, which in 1975 and even today, services smaller private aircraft lines.

I was able to eliminate Forest Lawn with the fact that it did not have a crematorium until 1986. The same went for Elmwood, Mt. Elliot, and Sacred Heart Cemetery, Meadowcrest Cemetery at Davison and Mound, and Gethsemane Cemetery on Gratiot. They did not have crematoriums in 1975. Woodlawn, next to Evergreen not only did not have any cremations anywhere near the infamous date, it was hardly ever used by Bagnasco Funeral Home to perform cremations.

Woodmere Cemetery in southwest Detroit had one cremation on July 30 1975, but the location of that cemetery and the funeral parlor associated with that cremation are quite a drive (twenty-seven miles round trip) from Beaverland and Grand River and then back all the way up to City Airport. For three guys trying to get out of town and back to New Jersey in time for dinner, that seems extremely out of the question. Frank Sheeran said that everything was going to be a straight shoot from everything else.

courtesy of www.jasonrichards.net

Conclusion

These are the facts. Frank Sheeran was one of the main suspects that the FBI listed as one of the men responsible for Hoffa's disappearance. He confessed to his lawyer Charles Brandt that he was the shooter and that the murder of Jimmy Hoffa took place at 17841 Beaverland Street in Detroit. After finally confirming his statements to Charles on videotape, he refused to eat and asked for a priest. He died a few weeks later. Had he lived, he would have faced an indictment for murder. No other person who has claimed to have killed Hoffa has ever given such detailed information about the drive from the Machus Red Fox to the location of the murder and then finally the method used to destroy the body.

Frank's statements that Hoffa was cremated with the assistance of a funeral home connected to the Detroit Mafia and that everything was finished an hour after Hoffa was murdered is information Frank directly received from Russell Bufalino.

Evergreen Cemetery is fifteen minutes away from the house on Beaverland and two cremations were performed that day. The entire operation was over in an hour and was conducted in broad daylight.

It is my opinion that the cremation of Hoffa's body was planned with the knowledge that Evergreen Cemetery had cremation ovens and a funeral parlor director with ties to the Detroit Outfit supplied the materials needed for the cremation. *"A funeral parlor in Detroit that the Detroit people were close to"* Frank said. All that funeral director had to do is have one of his unmarked Buick station wagons with a clamshell trunk with a box in the back and a fake burial transit permit on the dashboard or sun visor waiting in his parking lot. The two brothers identified by Frank Sheeran at the Beaverland house could have been dropped off at the funeral home, and got into the car. In the car were some overalls and baseball caps they could put on as to appear to be handy men or floor installers. Could be that they drove to the house around lunchtime and brought with them some linoleum flooring. Is it possible they were in and out of the house as to appear to neighbors that the lady that owned the place was having some work done while she was out of town?

This was all set up in advance and all the planners had to do was wait for Hoffa to take the bait and accept the offer of a meeting with Anthony Provenzano and Anthony Giacalone. Provenzano supplied the men to perform the clean up, and Giacalone with his connections

in the Detroit Outfit provided the materials and logistics. Once Hoffa saw that Frank Sheeran was in the car, he would have believed that his close ally for many years, Russell Bufalino was nearby and at the meeting. Frank Sheeran's statements to Charles Brandt regarding what happened to the body of Jimmy Hoffa are vague at first glance, but you have to wonder just how much he knew the area, and the other possible reasons for not telling
everything about the location where Hoffa's body was disposed of.

Could Evergreen's crematorium have been used for other off the books cremations without the knowledge of the cemetery workers?

One man can put to rest all of the rumors and theories. Thomas Andretta, of Las Vegas, Nevada, now in his seventies, will not give interviews regarding this case.

I hope the information I have gathered helps the public understand that after thirty-four years of investigation by the FBI and other law enforcement agencies, that Jimmy Hoffa's body will never be found. It is my belief that he was cremated at Evergreen Cemetery in Detroit.

On July 30 2009, all of the information in this book was turned over to the FBI Field Office in Detroit.

> Jeffry Scott Hansen
> August 2009

DIGGING FOR THE TRUTH 141

Appendix

To give the reader an understanding of the absolute hatred Jimmy Hoffa and Robert Kennedy had for each other, the following excerpts are from the actual transcripts of the McClellan Hearings. They are historical records of several such battles between the two men in the public forum. They have been edited only for length. If all of the transcripts between Hoffa and Robert Kennedy were put in this book, it would have been book one of five with just the testimony itself. The entire McClellan Hearings are over fifty volumes of testimony and evidence regarding the infiltration of organized crime into labor unions.

INVESTIGATION OF IMPROPER ACTIVITIES
IN THE LABOR OR MANAGEMENT FIELD
TUESDAY, AUGUST 20, 1957
United States Senate, Select Committee on Improper Activities In The Labor or Management Field, Washington D.C.

The select committee met at 10:30 a.m., pursuant to Senate Resolution 74, agreed to January 30, 1957, in the caucus room. Senate Office Building, Senator John L. McClellan (chairman of the select committee) Presiding.

Present: Senator John L. McClellan, Democrat, Arkansas; Senator Irving M. Ives, Republican, New York; **Senator John F. Kennedy**, Democrat, Massachusetts; Senator Pat McNamara, Democrat, Michigan; Senator Sam J. Ervin, Jr., Democrat,

North Janetina; Senator Karl E. Mundt, Republican, South Dakota; Senator Barry Goldwater. Republican, Arizona; Senator Carl T. Curtis, Republican, Nebraska. Also present: **Robert F. Kennedy, chief counsel**; Jerome S. Adlerman, chief assistant counsel; Paul J. Tierney, assistant counsel; Robert E. Dunne, assistant counsel; John Cye Cheasty, assistant counsel; Walter R. May, assistant counsel; Walter Sheridan, assistant counsel **K. Philip O'Donnell, assistant counsel**; Carmine S. Bellino, accounting consultant; **Pierre E. G. Salinger, investigator**; James Mundie, investigator; Ruth Young Watt, chief clerk. The Chairman: The committee will be in order.

The Chairman: The Chair observes that we have quite an audience this morning. You are welcome, but we must maintain order and bear that in mind. Be as comfortable as you can. This hearing will last possibly until 12 or 12:30 this morning. Is there anything at this time, Mr. Counsel?

Mr. Kennedy: No, sir.

The Chairman: Mr. Hoffa, will you be sworn, please?
You do solemnly swear that the evidence you shall give before this Senate select committee shall be the truth, the whole truth, and nothing but the truth, so help you God?

Mr. Hoffa: Yes; I do.

The Chairman: Mr. Hoffa, state your name

Mr. Fitzgerald: Mr. Chairman

The Chairman. The Chair will recognize you in a moment. State your name, your place of residence, and your business or occupation, please, sir.

Mr. Hoffa. My name is James R. Hoffa. I am a business representative and a vice president of the International Brotherhood of Teamsters.

The Chairman. Mr. Hoffa, you failed to give your address.

Mr. Hoffa. 16154 Robson, Detroit, Mich.

The Chairman. You have counsel to represent you?

Mr. Hoffa. Yes, sir, I do; George S. Fitzgerald, from Detroit.

The Chairman. Mr. Counsel, will you identify yourself for the record?

Mr. Fitzgerald. My name is George S. Fitzgerald, of Detroit, Mich., 2550 Guardian Building.

The Chairman: Thank you very much.
.
Are there any questions or comments by the members of the committee?

The Chairman. Thank you very much. All right, Mr. Counsel, you may proceed with the witness.

Mr. Kennedy. Mr. Hoffa, you have been in the teamsters union for how long?

Mr. Hoffa. In the teamsters union since approximately 1932.

Mr. Kennedy. And you were a president of a local at that time?

Mr. Hoffa. I was president of a local union, and I don't know whether it was local -32 or 34. I became president of a local union which was the Commission House Local Union which originated out of a Federal labor union.

Mr. Kennedy. Is that local 299?

Mr. Hoffa. No, it is not. I think it was 674, but don't hold me to the number.

Mr. Kennedy. Did it merge with 299?

Mr. Hoffa. No. 299 was a separate contract that had over-the road drivers, city cartage, and dock employees, and I was requested by the then secretary of the council through the international office to take over the operations of local 299 shortly thereafter.

Mr. Kennedy. When did you become president or head of 299?

Mr. Hoffa. Under trusteeship somewhere between 1932 and 1934 or 1935, somewhere around there.

Mr. Kennedy. Do you still hold a position with that union?

Mr. Hoffa. Yes, I was first appointed and then I have been elected several times since then.

Mr. Kennedy. Are you president of it?

Mr. Hoffa. That is correct.

Mr. Kennedy. Now, do you hold some other positions with the teamsters union at the present time?

Mr. Hoffa. Yes, sir; I do.

Mr. Kennedy. Could you tell us what they are?

Mr. Hoffa. Do you want them all, or the pertinent ones?

Mr. Kennedy. You are chairman of the negotiating committee?

Mr. Hoffa. I will give you the main ones and if you want more I will give them to you also. I am president of Joint Council 43, City of Detroit. I am president of Michigan Conference of Teamsters. I am president of the central conference of teamsters; chairman and president. I am vice president and negotiating chairman of the Central States Drivers Council. I am the coordinator of the Montgomery Ward national organizing drive. I am vice president of the international union. From time to time 1 have had several other designations, as assignments were given to me by the general president.

Mr. Kennedy. Since you have been with the teamsters union, you have been arrested a number of times; have you?

Mr. Hoffa. That is correct.

Mr. Kennedy. How many times, approximately, do you think?

Mr. Hoffa: **Well, I don't know, Bob. I haven't counted them up**. I think maybe about 17 times I have been picked up, took into custody of the police, and out of the 17 times, 3 of those times— in many instances these were dismissed——but in 3 of those times I received convictions.

Mr. Kennedy. Now, the first one was in 1940; was it?

Mr. Hoffa. I believe that was an assault and battery; is that correct?

Mr. Kennedy. That is not the one I was thinking of.

Mr. Hoffa. I am talking about the ones where I was simply taken off of a picket line because of a disagreement with some so-called policeman of authority without any legal authority. I haven't kept track of those.

Mr. Kennedy. But there are about 17 in all and you think you have been convicted on 3?

Mr. Hoffa. I think you have the record, and you can count them.

Mr. Kennedy. Then there was a violation of the Federal antitrust law.

Mr. Hoffa. There was indeed. But I want to point out that the violation of the Federal antitrust law resulted out of an organizing drive of wastepaper drivers in the city of Detroit. The result was that Thurman Arnold at that time was trying to interpret the law different than it is today, and we became involved with some employers of a small nature who refused to cooperate and attempt to establish decent wages and conditions for our members.

Mr. Kennedy. There was a charge that you knowingly engaged in a combination and conspiracy unreasonable to prevent other firms from selling wastepaper for shipment from Detroit and other States into Canada, wasn't that it?

Mr. Hoffa. It was settled on the basis of nolo contendere with a fine and probation, I believe.

Mr. Kennedy. There was a charge of a conspiracy between you, the union.

Mr. Hoffa. I want to correct the probation. There was just a fine originated out of that particular case, and strictly involved the question of labor.

Mr. Kennedy. A conspiracy between you or the union and certain wastepaper companies; is that correct?

Mr. Hoffa. It was so charged.

Mr. Kennedy. And it was nolo contendere?

Mr. Hoffa. Yes, sir.
Mr. Kennedy. And you paid a $1,000 fine?

Mr. Hoffa. Yes.

Mr. Kennedy. And then you were indicted in 1946, isn't that right, and convicted on a charge then?

Mr. Hoffa. For what purpose?

Mr. Kennedy. In connection with grocers and meat dealers in Detroit.

Mr. Hoffa. I was charged in a particular grand jury with a very serious charge.

Mr. Kennedy. That was of extortion?

Mr. Hoffa. That is correct. The extortion charge was a question of refusing to load nonunion individual owners who had taken jobs away from war veterans and refused to give those jobs back to the war veterans, because under OPA they had learned how to cheat on the question of paying the proper wage scales. Later on that was reduced to a simple misdemeanor of a Michigan State law known as the vine-trip law, and now the Michigan labor law.

Mr. Kennedy. You entered a plea on that?

Mr. Hoffa. That is correct ; a misdemeanor plea.

Mr. Kennedy. And nolo contendere?

Mr. Hoffa. No, a misdemeanor plea.

Mr. Kennedy. There was some money returned to the various companies, was there?

Mr. Hoffa. Moneys that we returned were the moneys that were collected in the way of initiation fees that had been paid by those individuals that made the complaint.

Mr. Kennedy. You were collecting $5 from each one of these grocers, as I understand it.

Mr. Hoffa. That is not correct,

Mr. Kennedy. Will you tell us?

Mr. Hoffa. We were collecting initiation fees from those grocers that were being entered into a ledger for the purpose of having initiation fees paid where they could have a paid-up book in the teamsters union.

Mr. Kennedy. And the court held that you shouldn't collect initiation fees.

Mr. Hoffa. The court didn't hold any such thing. The court held that we had violated the newly established State labor law, and since we had violated it, one of the agreements with the court was that we return the money. I may say for your information today that we have the right to do legally today what they said we could not do legally then.

Mr. Kennedy. You say you were collecting initiation fees and the court held that what you were doing was illegal?

Mr. Hoffa. The court held it was a violation of the Michigan labor law, but they did not hold, and if you would go into the case to look in all of the publicity, somebody had to save their face, so the result was that the court held it was a violation of a newly established law at that time, the Michigan State labor law.

DIGGING FOR THE TRUTH

Mr. Kennedy. Mr. Hoffa I am not saying whether you are guilty or not guilty. I am just trying to get

Mr. Hoffa. You are implying that I am guilty of extortion and it isn't true.

Mr. Kennedy. I asked you whether you were found guilty or whether you pleaded nolo contendere or whether you pleaded to a misdemeanor in 1946.

Mr. Hoffa. I have answered the question.

Mr. Kennedy. And that you had to return the money that you were collecting from these various grocers.
Mr. Hoffa. I have answered the question.

Mr. Kennedy. Approximately $7,500; is that right; that you had to return?

Mr. Hoffa. Approximately.

Mr. Kennedy. Now, in addition to these

Mr. Hoffa. I think maybe a little more.

Mr. Kennedy. Was it?

Mr. Hoffa. Yes.

Mr. Kennedy. The teamsters drive the trucks that you lease to them?

Mr. Hoffa. That is correct. Now, just a moment. Not that I lease. Let's correct the record.

Mr. Kennedy. Test Fleet.

Mr. Hoffa. Not that I lease.

Mr. Kennedy. Test Fleet.

Mr. Hoffa. Not that I lease.

Mr. Kennedy. That is fine. Test Fleet?

Mr. Hoffa. Yes.

Mr. Kennedy. The company was set up in the name of Mr. Wrape and then, I believe, the officers and the stockholders originally were a couple of the assistants, two of the attorneys from Mr. Wrape's office?

Mr. Hoffa. I think, maybe, you are right.

Mr. Kennedy. Then the stock was transferred, was it, down to Tennessee?

Mr. Hoffa. I think you are right.

Mr. Kennedy. Who was the stock transferred to?

Mr. Hoffa. Josephine Poszywak and Alice Johnson.

Mr. Kennedy. Who is Poszywak?

Mr. Hoffa. My wife is Josephine Poszywak, and Alice Johnson is Bert Brennen's wife.

Mr. Kennedy, You selected the maiden names of your wives?

Mr. Hoffa. The attorneys advised that.

Mr. Kennedy. Why?

Mr. Hoffa. For the purpose of not involving them in the lawsuits that I become involved in as a labor representative.

Mr. Kennedy. They thought it was better?

Mr. Hoffa. I think that was the explanation. I don't recall it, offhand.

Mr. Kennedy. You got rid of your equipment, as I understand it, the trucks and trailers that you had from National Equipment Co. Did you have some difficulty getting trucks and trailers leased to Commercial Carriers?

Mr. Hoffa. You don't have any difficulty at any time buying trucks or trailers.

Mr. Kennedy. Where did you get your trucks and trailers?

Mr. Hoffa. I got them through Commercial Carriers, at the same discount price everybody else gets them who has trucks working for Commercial Carriers.

Mr. Kennedy. So, Commercial Carriers had this difficulty up in Pontiac, was it?

Mr. Hoffa. No ; it was not. It was Flint.

Mr. Kennedy. Flint, Mich. Their attorneys set this company up for your wife and for Bert Brennan's wife, and then they arranged to get the equipment for you, did they?

(The witness conferred with his counsel.)

Mr. Hoffa. Let's straighten the record out. I told you that Jim Wrape was an attorney. I think you are an attorney. It is my understanding an attorney can have more than one client. Because he represents a client other than the second client doesn't necessarily mean that you should refer to him as the client of the company. Rather, you should refer to him as the lawyer for Test Fleet.

Mr. Kennedy. Did you ever pay him, Mr. Hoffa?

Mr. Hoffa. I, personally, did not pay him, and I don't know whether or not the corporation did.

Mr. Kennedy. Did your wife pay him?

Mr. Hoffa. I don't know.

Mr. Kennedy. Did Bert Brennan's wife pay him?

Mr. Hoffa. I don't know. I can get the information, if you desire it.

Mr. Kennedy. So, you got the equipment from Commercial Carriers. How were you able to pay for the equipment?

Mr. Hoffa. Out of earnings, after the down payment.

Mr. Kennedy. Where did you get the down payment?

Mr. Hoffa. I believe, if I am not mistaken—it is a matter again of recollection—that it came out of the sale of National Equipment.

TESTIMONY BY JAMES R. HOFFA THAT CAME LATER THAT DAY

Mr. Kennedy. Has this been a profitable operation?

Mr. Hoffa. You have the record. I. think you could say that it was.

Mr. Kennedy. Well, I am asking you the question.

Mr. Hoffa. Since it is not my company, I can only say that I think that it was.

Mr. Kennedy. It was. You do not know. Your wife has not let you know how much money she made?

Mr. Hoffa. I think I know how much she made.

Mr. Kennedy. Approximately, how much do you think she made in that company since it was set up?

Mr. Hoffa. I can't tell you, offhand, but a guess. I can give it to you this afternoon, if I can get it.

Mr. Kennedy. We have some figures here.

Mr. Hoffa. **Read them off. Brother.**

Mr. Kennedy: November 15, 1949, $4,000 each to Mrs. Hoffa and Mrs. Brennan in their maiden names. In December of 1950, $15,000 each. In October of 1951, $3,500 each. In July of 1952, $5,000 each. In December of 1952, $5,000 each. In January of 1954, $10,000 each. April of 1955, $5,000 each. In June of 1955, $5,000 each. Was that corporation Test Fleet—does it, also, have another name?

Mr. Hoffa. I think that today it is called Hobren Corp.

Mr. Kennedy. Hobren Corp.?

Mr. Hoffa. I believe that is correct.

Mr. Kennedy. We understand that they, also, in addition to the moneys that I mentioned, purchased some land. Test Fleet; is that right.
Mr. Hoffa. That is right.

Mr. Kennedy. How much money did that land cost?

Mr. Hoffa. I think $20,000, rather than take the dividends.

Mr. Kennedy. So, in addition to what I have mentioned, that is $5,000 down on October 1, 1955, and $15,000 down in 1956. That makes a total payment to your wife in her maiden name and Mrs. Brennan in her maiden name of $125,000.

Mr. Hoffa. Before taxes.

Mr. Kennedy. Does that seem right, before taxes?

Mr. Hoffa: Before taxes.

Mr. Kennedy. You have to pay taxes on that?

Mr. Hoffa. I would assume everybody does.

Mr. Kennedy. So, that is through 1956. That is with how much investment originally?

Mr. Hoffa. It was an investment, I believe, of $4,000, with a commitment of $50,000 in case the business went wrong, which they would have to pay. So it was, actually, an investment of $54,000.

Mr. Kennedy. Who was the commitment to?

Mr. Hoffa. To the bank.

Mr. Hoffa. Mr. Chairman, I would like to answer that as a direct question, but again I am reminded in my own mind, listening to statements that have been made in this committee, attributed to myself, by other people, which I can't recall, and I have to say to the best of my recollection I cannot recall anybody being assigned or going into any grand jury chambers, and I may say, sir, that a certain judge that conducted that vigorously denied it when it appeared in the newspaper.

The Chairman. Let me ask you one more time. If you did this, this is certainly something you would not forget, unless you were in such a habit of it, and it has become such a habit, you could not remember it at that particular time, and there is no evidence here to indicate that.

The Chairman. Did you not procure these Minifons for the purpose of, and did you not use them to place on witnesses who went before the grand jury, so that when they came out you would have a recording of the testimony they had given?

Mr. Hoffa. May I consult with my attorney, sir?

DIGGING FOR THE TRUTH

The Chairman. Yes, sir.

(The witness conferred with his counsel.)

The Chairman. Let us have order.

Mr. Hoffa. Mr. Chairman, I must say to the best of my recollection, I did not assign, nor direct anybody to do any such a thing, but because of stories appearing in the paper, which I don't have any knowledge of, and cannot recall from memory, I must make the statement I am making, sir. If you have something to refresh my memory, I will be glad to try and help you, sir.

The Chairman. I have done as much to refresh your memory as I know how to do. If you cannot recall it from that, and you want to leave the record that way, if you want to think that this committee is so stupid and that the public is so stupid that they will believe that you could not remember having done a thing like that, you leave the record that way.

The Chairman: Proceed, Mr. Counsel.

Mr. Kennedy: Mr. Hoffa, can you refresh your recollection at all now in connection with this, or in connection with anything, if Mr. Dio made any arrangements to send people out to your headquarters in Detroit?

Mr. Hoffa. To the best of my recollection, I must recall on my memory, I cannot remember.

Mr. Kennedy. "To the best of my recollection I must recall on my memory that I cannot remember", is that your answer?

Mr. Hoffa. That is right. I cannot remember anybody being sent there.

The Chairman. Let us have order.

Mr. Kennedy. Could I try to refresh his recollection, Mr. Chairman, again? We are almost running out of refreshers, Mr. Hoffa.

Mr. Hoffa. Well, sir, I am trying to help. This is a serious situation.

The Chairman: What is that about,

Mr. Hoffa I

(The witness conferred with his counsel.)

Mr. Hoffa: Well, apparently it was something I was having done, and I cannot recollect from this telephone call exactly what it was. I can probably check up and maybe I can inquire around as to what it was, but at this particular moment I cannot give you the answer.

The Chairman. Mr. Hoffa, you have been continuously asking us to refresh your memory.

Mr. Hoffa. That is right, sir.

The Chairman. Can you tell us how we can do it?

Mr. Hoffa. Well, sir

The Chairman. How? After all, are you still taking the position that your memory has failed you?

Mr. Hoffa. I don't say my memory has failed, but I say to the best of my recollection, I cannot recall the substance of this telephone call, nor place the facts together concerning what it pertains to.

The Chairman. But if these things do not refresh your memory, it would take the power of God to do it. The instrumentalities of mankind, obviously, are not adequate. Proceed.

Mr. Kennedy. It doesn't refresh your recollection? They are the best ; they work for the U. N. and everywhere else? Listen to this carefully—
And wherever you want to need 'em, any part of the country if you want to find out they're your people, you let me know.

Mr. Kennedy: What does that mean? If you want to find out they're your people you let me know? What does that mean? Who are these people?

Mr. Hoffa. Well, Mr. Kennedy, I realize what the Chair just said, but I still must say to the best of my recollection, I cannot recall what that paragraph you read means at this time. I cannot recall it.

Mr. Kennedy. Mr. Hoffa, it is just beyond the powers of comprehension that you can't recall that. A reasonable man cannot believe you when you say that you can't recall that.

(The witness conferred with his counsel.)

Mr. Hoffa. Well, I would say this to you. I just don't have a normal situation here in regards to the occupation I am in. I have strikes, I have people visiting me, meetings, telephone calls, and a hundred and one things. I cannot, to the best of my recollection, give you an answer to what this pertains to.

Mr. Kennedy: **You have had the worst case of amnesia in the last two days I have ever heard of.**

The Chairman. Let us have order.

Mr. Hoffa: I say to the best of my recollection I do not recall the situation.

****

TUESDAY, AUGUST 5, 1958

It is in this session that Hoffa is not only questioned by Robert Kennedy, but also by his brother Senator John F. Kennedy. It is noted that Senator Frank Church was at the hearing on this day. In 1975 he would chair his own committee, which investigated the Central Intelligence Agency's attempts to assassinate foreign leaders, including Patrice Lumumba of the Congo, Rafael Trujillo of the Dominican Republic, the Diem brothers of Vietnam, Gen. René Schneider of Chile and President John F. Kennedy's plan to use the Mafia to kill Fidel Castro of Cuba. Sam Giancana of the Chicago Outfit was to testify but was killed just days before he was called to the hearings. Hoffa was also going to testify in those 1975 hearings but disappeared before he had the chance.

United States Senate, Select Committee on Improper Activities in The Labor or Management Field, Washington, D.C. Present : Senator John L. McClellan, Democrat, Arkansas, **Senator John F. Kennedy**, Democrat, Massachusetts; **Senator Frank Church**, Democrat Idaho ; Senator Irving M. Ives, Republican, New York ; Senator E. Mundt, Republican, South Dakota ; Senator Carl T. Curtis, Republican, Nebraska. Also present: **Robert F. Kennedy**, chief counsel; assistant counsel; John J. McGovern, assistant counsel; Pierre E. Salinger, investigator

On the basis of previous testimony before this committee, replete with improper practices and conduct on the part of Mr. Hoffa and some of his associates, a serious question has arisen in the minds of the committee as to Mr. Hoffa's motivation and the direction and leadership he proposes to give this great and important union.

As spelled out in the committee's interim report, the evidence had shown that in numerous instances Mr. Hoffa has aligned himself with certain underworld characters, who are a part and parcel of the criminal elements and most sinister forces in this country.

When he testified before the committee, Mr. Hoffa said he would attempt to divest himself of some of his associations and give this union the character and quality of leadership and administration worthy of the importance and high purposes of this great labor organization.

In these hearings the committee will be interested in ascertaining whether he has been successful — or what efforts and progress he has made in that direction. It will be recalled that when Mr. Hoffa testified before, he suffered seriously from 'lack of memory," and thus avoided answering many pertinent questions seeking information, about which he had knowledge and in which the committee was interested. It is to be hoped that his memory has improved and that he can now give the committee the cooperation and assistance it is entitled to receive and that he, as an American citizen and the leader of this great union, is under obligation to give. This series of hearings will not be of 1 day's duration. The affairs of this union and its top officers are so intricate and complex that it may well engage the attention of the committee here in public hearings for several weeks. Mr. Hoffa will be expected to remain here during that time to answer all pertinent questions, to give explanations, or to refute any testimony the committee may hear of improper practices, or that which may be derogatory to him personally. We have a right to expect from him candid and truthful answers. For him to do less would seriously compromise his position and cast further doubt upon his integrity and the propriety of his union leadership, I believe Mr. Hoffa observed recently in Seattle, Washington that the Teamsters have the power to shut down the economy of this Nation at its will. That I think we can concede. Any union in which such tremendous power is reposed also bears equal obligation and responsibility to the people and to the Government of the United States. It is unthinkable that the leaders of any such powerful organization should have an alliance or understanding in any area of its activities with racketeers, gangsters, and hoodlums. Such an alliance or any working arrangements with such characters and elements places a dangerous force at the jugular vein of America's economic life.

The committee is convinced that the great mass — the million and a half members of the Teamsters Union — are honest, law-abiding citizens. The committee is interested in serving them — in protecting their interest and their welfare.

The committee is also interested in ascertaining the truth regarding policies, activities, and practices associated with this union and its leadership and with labor-management relations generally that

need to be corrected or prohibited. To that end the committee seeks information with a view of submitting recommendations to the Congress for appropriate remedial legislation. Notwithstanding Mr. Hoffa's reported remarks of contempt for this committee, its source of authority, the United States Senate, and the purposes and objectives for which the committee labors, the committee will pursue its duty and carry out the mandate in the resolution creating it. In this, we hope to have, and have every right to expect, Mr. Hoffa's cooperation and assistance. This is something he owes to the great mass of working people, dues-paying members whose interest he is supposed to represent, whose welfare he is supposed to promote, and whose rights he is
duty bound to protect.

The committee shall now proceed as faithfully and diligently in the course herein set forth as it is within its capacity to do so.

Senator Ives. Mr. Chairman, before you start, I would like to commend you upon that statement. It is an excellent presentation. I think it expresses the feeling of every single one of us. Before we get through with this series of hearings, at which Mr. Hoffa will be present, I have a few questions I expect to ask him.

The Chairman. Thank you. Senator Ives.

Are there any other comments?

Senator Curtis?

Senator Curtis. No statement.

The Chairman. Senator Kennedy?

Senator John F Kennedy. No statement.

The Chairman. Thank you very much.

Mr. Hoffa, will you be sworn, please, sir? You do solemnly swear that the evidence you give before this Senate select committee shall be the truth, the whole truth and nothing but the truth, so help you God?

Mr. Hoffa. I do.

The Chairman. State your name, your place of residence, and your business or occupation.

Mr. Hoffa. My name is James R. Hoffa, 16154 Robson, Detroit, Mich., and I am president of the International Brotherhood of Teamsters, Chauffeurs, Warehousemen, and Helpers of America.

The Chairman. You have counsel.

Mr. Counsel, identify yourself.

Mr. Hoffa. Yes, sir, I have counsel today, and I desire my counsel to make a statement prior to the hearing also.

The Chairman. And not as counsel for the union. All right, with that record straightened out now, we may proceed.

Mr. Kennedy. Mr. Hoffa, did you know Mr. Joseph Holtzman?

Mr. Hoffa. Yes, I did.

Mr. Kennedy. He was a close friend of yours, was he?

Mr. Hoffa. I knew Joe Holtzman.

Mr. Kennedy. He was a close friend of yours?

Mr. Hoffa. I knew Joe Holtzman.

Mr. Kennedy. He was a close friend of yours?
Mr. Hoffa. I knew Joe Holtzman.

Mr. Kennedy. He was a close friend of yours?

Mr. Hoffa. Just a moment. I knew Joe Holtzman, and he wasn't any particular friend of mine.

Mr. Kennedy. Just answer the Question.

DIGGING FOR THE TRUTH 169

The Chairman: Let us start off right here. This is public business. The question is whether he was a close friend seems proper, and you know a lot of people who may not be close friends, and may just barely be acquaintances. In order to show the association and throw light on testimony that may be forthcoming, it is quite proper the witness to answer as to his acquaintanceship, whether it is one of friendship or one of business association, or any other pertinent factor that might help us to evaluate testimony as we proceed. Go ahead, Mr. Counsel.

Mr. Kennedy. Was he a close friend of yours?

Mr. Hoffa. I say he was an acquaintance.

Mr. Kennedy. An acquaintance?

Mr. Hoffa. Yes, sir.

Mr. Kennedy. You used to visit with him?

Mr. Hoffa. Occasionally.

Mr. Kennedy. And he came to visit you?

Mr. Hoffa. Occasionally.

Mr. Kennedy. "What was his business, Mr. Hoffa?

Mr. Hoffa. He had a dry-cleaning concern, and he was a labor- relations consultant.

Mr. Kennedy. How long have you known him, or had you known
him?

Mr. Hoffa. Probably since 1934.

Mr. Kennedy. Did he have a partner?

Mr. Hoffa. Yes.
Mr. Kennedy. What was the partner's name?

Mr. Hoffa. Jack Bushkin.

Mr. Kennedy. Is he still alive?

Mr. Hoffa. Yes.

Mr. Kennedy. He is a friend of yours?

Mr. Hoffa. Yes.
Mr. Kennedy. Is he a close friend of yours?

Mr. Hoffa. An acquaintance.

Mr. Kennedy. Just an acquaintance?

Mr. Hoffa. He is a person that I know and he is a friend, but a friendly acquaintance.

Mr. Kennedy. A friendly acquaintance?

Mr. Hoffa. Yes, sir.

Mr. Kennedy. Did you visit with him occasionally?

Mr. Hoffa. Yes, sir.

Mr. Kennedy. And he visited with you occasionally?

Mr. Hoffa. Yes, sir.

Mr. Kennedy. Mr. Holtzman and Mr. Bushkin were in this labor relations business together; were they?

Mr. Hoffa. I believe they were.

Mr. Kennedy. Did you ever discuss any contracts with them?

Mr. Hoffa. I certainly did.

Mr. Kennedy. You did on occasion?

Mr. Hoffa. That is right.

Mr. Kennedy. Did you negotiate any contracts with them?

Mr. Hoffa. That is right.

Mr. Kennedy. You did do that?

Mr. Hoffa. Yes, sir.

Mr. Kennedy. Did you receive any money from Mr. Holtzman?

Mr. Hoffa. I borrowed money from Holtzman and Bushkin both.

Mr. Kennedy. When was this?

Mr. Hoffa. I believe I will have to refer to the record because I Testified to that the last time I was here— did you say "when"?

Mr. Kennedy. Yes.

Mr. Hoffa. Some time in 1952 or 1953.

Mr. Kennedy. How much money did you receive?
Mr. Hoffa: $5,000.

Mr. Kennedy. From each one?

Mr. Hoffa. That is correct.

Mr. Kennedy. And I believe the record shows that that was in cash that you got from them?

Mr. Hoffa. That is correct.

Mr. Kennedy. And that there was no note on it?

Mr. Hoffa. That is correct.

Mr. Kennedy. And did you pay them both back?

Mr. Hoffa. I did.

Mr. Kennedy. And there was no interest paid?

Mr. Hoffa. That is right.

Mr. Kennedy. So they at least were close enough friends that they would loan you money without interest in cash and without any evidence that there was in fact a loan is that correct?

Mr. Hoffa. They did.

Mr. Kennedy. Now, do you know or did you know Mr. John Paris?
Mr. Hoffa. I did.

Mr. Kennedy. How long ago did he die?

Mr. Hoffa. Three or four years.

Mr. Kennedy. How long had you known him?

Mr. Hoffa. Probably 15 or more years, 10 or 15 years or more.

Mr. Kennedy. You were a close friend of his?

Mr. Hoffa. Not necessarily.

Mr. Kennedy. Did he used to visit you?

Mr. Hoffa. You mean at home?

Mr. Kennedy. Yes.

Mr. Hoffa. I don't think that he ever did.

Mr. Kennedy. He was a business agent of the Laundry Workers' Union, was he?

Mr. Hoffa. That is right.

Mr. Kennedy. He was married to a woman by the name of Sylvia?

Mr. Hoffa. Yes, sir.
Mr. Kennedy. She is a friend of you and your family?

Mr. Hoffa. That is right.

Mr. Kennedy. And they have a son?

Mr. Hoffa. That is right.

Mr. Kennedy. What is his name?

Mr. Hoffa. Charles O'Brien.

Mr., Kennedy. And he is with your union, is he?

Mr. Hoffa. That is right.

Mr. Kennedy, He used to be with the Retail Clerks' Union?

Mr. Hoffa, That is right.

Mr. Kennedy. And the Retail Clerks' Union had its headquarters in the Teamsters' Buildings?
Mr. Hoffa. That is right.

Mr. Kennedy. In Detroit?

Mr. Hoffa. Yes, sir.

Mr. Kennedy. And he is now working for your union, local 299?

Mr. Hoffa. That is right.

Mr. Kennedy. He is a business agent for 299?

Mr. Hoffa. That is right.

Mr. Kennedy. Now, on Mr. Holtzman and Mr. Bushkin, did they represent on any occasion the Detroit Institute of Laundry?

Mr. Hoffa. They may have, and I believe they did.

Mr. Kennedy. Did you have some discussions with them about that?

Mr. Hoffa. I don't think that I discussed it with them.

Mr. Kennedy. Did you discuss the Detroit Institute of Laundry with Mr. Holtzman?

Mr. Hoffa. I may have.

Mr. Kennedy. Can you remember that?

Mr. Hoffa. No; I don't.

Mr. Kennedy. You don't remember?

Mr. Hoffa. No; I don't.

Mr. Kennedy. In 1949, did they make arrangements for you to visit with any of the representatives of the Detroit Institute of Laundry?

Mr. Hoffa. I don't know whether they did or not, and I met some representatives of the laundry and I don't know who arranged the meeting.

Mr. Kennedy. You don't know how that was arranged?

Mr. Hoffa. No.

Mr. Kennedy. What did they come to see you about?

Mr. Hoffa. With the question of the dispute between their organization and our organization.

Mr. Kennedy. Could you tell us about .what conversations you had with them?

Mr. Hoffa. Well, how long ago was that?

Mr. Kennedy. I said 1949.

Mr. Hoffa. I believe that the contract was open for negotiations, and there arose a question between the employers and our union as to whether or not there was a right to strike or a necessity to arbitrate the differences when they couldn't agree.

Mr. Kennedy. This is not then, this is back in 1949. That was in 1951 when there was a question about that. That is when the contract was up for renewal, and I believe the man conducting the negotiations was Mr. Isaac Litwak, of Local 295 of the Teamsters.

Mr. Hoffa. Let us go back a step. You have asked me whether or not Holtzman had ever talked to me about the question of the laundry institute?

Mr. Kennedy. Yes.

Mr. Hoffa. To the best of my knowledge the only time that I ever knew Holtzman was engaged or involved in any way with the laundry institute was the one incident where he was involved Avitli Litwak.

Mr. Kennedy. In 1951?

Mr. Hoffa. That could have been, and I am not sure of the date.

Mr. Kennedy. Did they come to see you on two different occasions then, the representatives of the Detroit Institute of Laundry?

Mr., Hoffa. I don't know if it was once or twice, and they did come to see me.

Mr. Kennedy. Going back to 1949 when the contract was up, and Mr. Litwak was negotiating the contract, do you remember they came to see you on that occasion?

Mr. Hoffa. I think that your facts are wrong. I think when they came to see me there was a question involving the contract as to whether or not he could strike because I believe, and this is only from me, there were certain sections open for negotiations. When they got into a deadlock, I believe it was a question whether they could strike
or had to arbitrate. And I don't recall any other incident that I discussed with them.

Mr. Kennedy. Mr. Hoffa, all I asked you was whether in 1949, when this contract was up, and there were negotiations going on between Mr. Isaac Litwak and this representative of the Detroit Institute of Laundry, they came to visit you on that occasion.

Mr. Hoffa. I say they came to visit me, and the best I can recall was one contract. Whether it was the one you mentioned first or the second one, I don't recall but it seems to me that the question involved, as I stated before.

Mr. Kennedy. We have gone through that, and it was a 3-year contract. Let me see if this refreshes your recollection. It was a 3-year contract, I believe, signed in 1949, and in 1951 there was a question, as you explained, as to whether local 285 could strike. I believe that they came to see you on that occasion for you to make a determination

Mr. Hoffa. They told me they were coming down to testify.

Senator Kennedy. They called you?

Mr. Hoffa. No. I met them at the airport. I did not even know they were going to be on the same plane.

Senator Kennedy. Why did you raise the matter of Holtzman?

Mr. Hoffa. Why did I raise the matter with Holtzman?

Senator Kennedy. Of Holtzman?

Mr. Hoffa. Maybe they did. I don't know.

Senator Kennedy. You don't recall?

Mr. Hoffa. No, I don't.

Senator Kennedy. Who was it you talked to?

Mr. Hoffa. I think both Meissen and Balkwill was there. But I think it was in a kidding way. I don't think we made any serious discussion concerning this problem. As a matter of fact, I know we did not.

Mr. Kennedy. **Mr. Hoffa, after the hearing was over on Tuesday, while leaving the hearings after these people had testified regarding this matter, did you say, "That S. O. B., I'll break his back"?**

Mr. Hoffa. **Who?**

Mr. Kennedy. **You.**

Mr. Hoffa. **Say it to who?**

Mr. Kennedy. To anyone. Did you make that statement after these people testified before this committee?

Mr. Hoffa. I never talked to either one of them after they testified.

Mr. Kennedy. I am not talking about them. Did you make that statement here in the hearing room after the testimony was finished?

Mr. Hoffa. Not concerning them, as far as I know.

Mr. Kennedy. Who did you make it about, then?

Mr. Hoffa. I don't know. I may have been discussing someone in a figure of speech. I don't even remember it.

Mr. Kennedy. Whose back were you going to break, Mr. Hoffa?

Mr. Hoffa. It was a figure of speech. I don't know what you are talking about. .

Mr. Kennedy. I am trying to find out whose back you were trying to break.

Mr. Hoffa. It is a figure of speech.

Mr. Kennedy. What?

Mr. Hoffa. A figure of speech.

Mr. Kennedy. A figure of speech about what?

Mr. Hoffa. I don't know.

Mr. Kennedy. Who were you talking about?

Mr. Hoffa. I have no knowledge of what you are talking about.

Mr. Kennedy. Do you deny that you made the statement?

Mr. Hoffa. I don't recall making it.

Mr. Kennedy. Do you deny that you made it?

Mr. Hoffa. I could have made a remark to somebody we had been talking about the day before or the day after.

It is a figure of speech.

Mr. Kennedy. Whose back were you going to break?

Mr. Hoffa. It does not mean physically.

Mr. Kennedy. Let's find out whose back you were going to break figuratively.

Mr. Hoffa. I don't know. I don't know.

The Chairman. Let me ask you this question: Whether physically or figuratively

Mr. Hoffa. What, sir?

The Chairman (continuing) . Did you make that remark about any
member of this committee, any member of its staff, or any witness who may have testified before it or whose testimony is expected?

Mr. Hoffa. I do not recall making any such a statement. I certainly did not make it about any member of this committee or any staff member or any witness that I can recall. I know I did not. I am sure of that.

The Chairman. You certainly could recall back to Monday.

Mr. Hoffa. I can't recall making any such statement, sir.

The Chairman. All right. Proceed, Mr. Kennedy.

Mr. Kennedy. I would like to call a witness, Mr. Chairman.

Mr. Williams. Are we excused?

The Chairman. No, You may remain where you are. There is one point we want to clear up, and see if we can refresh Mr. Hoffa's memory a bit.

Mr. Kennedy, Mr. Roberts,

The Chairman, Be sworn, please. You do solemnly swear the evidence you shall give before this Senate select committee shall be the truth, the whole truth, and nothing but the truth, so help you God?

Mr. Roberts. I do.

The Chairman, State your name, your place of residence, and your present employment,

Mr. Roberts. My name is Robert D, Roberts. I live at 120 C Street NE. I am a member of the Capitol Police force.

The Chairman, You live here in the city of Washington?

Mr. Roberts, Yes, sir; I do.

The Chairman, Where is your home?

Mr. Roberts, My home is Jefferson City, Mo.

The Chairman. Jefferson City, Mo.?

Mr. Roberts. Originally, yes, sir.

The Chairman. How long have you been in Washington?

Mr. Roberts. About a year and a half, sir.

The Chairman. How long have you been on the Capitol Police force?

Mr. Roberts. A year June 7.

The Chairman. A year June 7?

Mr. Roberts. Yes, sir.

The Chairman. You waive counsel? You know you are entitled to have an attorney present, if you desire.

Mr. Roberts. Yes, sir.

The Chairman. All right, Mr. Kennedy. Proceed.

Mr., Kennedy. You are a member of the Capitol Police?

Mr. Roberts. That is right, sir.

Mr. Kennedy. You have been a member how long?

Mr. Roberts. One year June 7.

Mr. Kennedy. You were on duty, were you, on Tuesday in this hearing room, of this week?

Mr. Roberts, Tuesday ; yes, sir, I was on duty here in the hearing room,

Mr., Kennedy. Mr. Roberts, you were on duty at the end of the session, were you?

Mr. Roberts. Yes, sir; until the session was over. I stayed here until the area was cleared.

Mr. Kennedy. Did you hear a statement made by the witness, Mr. Hoffa?
Mr. Roberts. Yes, sir ; not in this room, though,

Mr., Kennedy. Where was the statement made?

Mr. Roberts. On the street.

Mr. Roberts. After the session was over, then I went downstairs, and from there I was to perform the rest of my duties outside, in front of the entrance of Delaware and C Streets, right by the trolley-car tracks. I was standing there, and that is where I overheard the statement.

The Chairman. Speak a little louder.

Mr. Kennedy. Would you tell the committee what he stated, what Mr. Hoffa stated, putting blanks in where blanks are necessary. First, would you write it out, and then would you make the statement?

Mr. Roberts. You want me to write it out, leaving out the profanity?

Mr. Kennedy. No; just state what he said and leave out the profanity. Then I will have you write it out.

Mr. Roberts. He said, "That sneaky little 'blank' I'll break his back". I have no way of knowing what he was talking about or who he was referring to. It was just that one statement that I heard.

The Chairman. Had he just left the hearing room here?

Mr. Roberts. I presume so.

The Chairman. Had we just adjourned?

Mr. Roberts. Yes. It was very soon after adjournment.

Senator Curtis. Mr. Chairman?

The Chairman. Senator Curtis.

Senator Curtis. To whom did he make the statement?

Mr. Roberts. He was talking to this gentleman that was with him.

Senator Curtis. Do you know who he was?

Mr. Roberts. I am not sure who he was. I think I know who he was, but I am not sure. I could identify the man, but I don't know if this is his name. I think it was Mr. Fitzgerald.

Senator Curtis. Do you know about whom he made the statement?

Mr. Roberts. I have no idea, sir. I only heard that one statement; that is all.

Senator Curtis. Do you know what subject matter was under discussion when he made the statement?

Mr. Roberts. I have no idea, sir ; none whatsoever.

The Chairman. Now write out the statement so that it may be incorporated into the record.

Mr. Roberts. Verbatim, sir?

The Chairman. Write it verbatim.

Mr. Kennedy. Does that refresh your recollection, Mr. Hoffa?

Mr. Hoffa. It doesn't refresh my recollection. We may have been discussing some situation, and I may have said that.

The Chairman. The important thing in this, and I don't know nor does anyone else, is whether you were directing those remarks to any member of this committee, any member of its staff, or any witness who had testified or whose testimony the committee expected to receive. That is the point.

Mr. Hoffa: You can rest assured it was not.

The Chairman. You can state unequivocally under oath you were not referring either physically or figuratively to any of those whom I have identified?

Mr. Hoffa. I did not.

The Chairman. Proceed, Mr. Kennedy.

Mr. Kennedy. Mr. Hoffa, we had some testimony before this committee regarding Mr. Milton Holt, secretary-treasurer of local 805, in New York. Could you tell us whether you have taken any steps

Mr. Williams. Mr. Chairman, may I see what the witness wrote out?

The Chairman. Yes; you may. I cannot permit it to be verbally stated in the language in which it is written over the air or before this audience.

Mr. Williams. You can go ahead with the examination.

Mr. Kennedy. Mr. Hoffa, we have had testimony regarding Mr. Milton Holt, secretary-treasurer of local 805.

Mr. Hoffa. Yes?

Mr. Kennedy. O. K.

Mr. Hoffa. Sure. Go ahead.
Mr. Kennedy. Secretary-treasurer of local 805, Mr. Hoffa.

Mr. Hoffa. What about it?

Mr. Kennedy. Have you taken any steps against Mr. Milton Holt?

Mr. Hoffa. I have not. The man is indicted, waiting trial. He was found guilty of an antitrust, the same as all the employers who are involved with him. I have discussed the matter with him. But I have taken no action.

Mr. Kennedy. You have taken no steps to have him removed from his position?

Mr. Hoffa. I have not.

Mr. Kennedy. He is very close and was identified as being very close to Johnnie Dioguardi before this committee.

Mr., Hoffa. Is that a question?

Mr. Kennedy. You have still taken no steps against him?

Mr. Hoffa. No.

Mr. Kennedy. He was involved also in the so-called bouncing charter, where this charter bounced around from one individual to another, according to the testimony before our committee; that he was very close to Mr. Johnnie Dioguardi and Mr. Getlin, in that matter. Can you tell us whether you looked into that at all?

Mr. Hoffa. I think I have talked to Milton Holt concerning the problem. His case is coming up in court. We will take proper action at that time if necessary.

Mr. Kennedy. You have taken no steps against him?

Mr. Kennedy. On Al Reger, even if he had not been convicted, here are some of his associates as developed by the committee. Mr. Berl Michelson, who has a criminal record; Harry Davidoff, about whom we have extensive testimony ; Ralph Mahone. Tony "Ducks" Corallo, Johnny Dioguardi, Carmine Formandi, Dickey Miksky, all of whom have criminal records; Abe (alias, Archie Cates, Sam Davy, Milton Hope. This man himself was a member of the Communist Party from 1918 until at least the late 1940's. He was a member of the" Daily Worker Advisory Council. He is press director of the New York County Communist Party. He was convicted in 1957 of extortion, and he is still a union official. It is in a union that is controlled, according to the testimony before the committee, by Tony "Ducks" Corallo. You still have not taken any steps against him? Are you frightened of these people, Mr. Hoffa?

Mr. Hoffa. I am not frightened of anybody, Mr. Kennedy, and I don't intend to have the impression left, as has been stated publicly, that I am controlled by gangsters. I am not controlled by them but by the same token I do not intend to go around and evade the provisions of the constitution of the international union which you accused Mr.

Beck of doing by having dictatorial powers. I want to be able to follow the constitution in due time. This situation will be cleared up. If you recall I took office almost just about February 1. Then I went through a long trial in New York which tied me up. I had the question of monitors which tied me up. I have not had much opportunity to do the normal duties that would have taken place if all of the various incidents had not come about during my short period of time as general president. In due time these situations will be cleared up.

(At this point, members of the committee Present were: Senators McClellan, Ives, Ervin, Church, Kennedy, Mundt, and Curtis.)

Mr. Kennedy. Mr. Hoffa, that would make a great deal of sense. I would be very sympathetic if it were not for the fact that a majority of these people are in the Central States Conference, and people under your jurisdiction. You have people in Detroit, at least 15, who have police records. You have Joey Glimco, in Chicago. I say you are not tough enough to get rid of these people, then.

Mr. Hoffa. I don't propose to be tough.

Mr. Kennedy. You haven't moved against any of them.

Mr. Hoffa. I don't propose to act tough. I will follow the constitution of the international union.

In due time the situation, where necessary, will be corrected.

Mr. Kennedy. Why haven't you gotten rid of any of these people in the Central States Conference, and why are these people allowed to continue with police records, Mr. Hoffa?

Mr. Hoffa. If there are no charges filed against them.

Mr. Kennedy. Why don't you take action against them yourself?

Mr. Hoffa. I told you why.

Mr. Kennedy. Why haven't you taken action in the Central States Conference against these people during all this period of time.

Joey Glimco has been in there for 10 or 15 years. He has 38 arrests.

Mr. Hoffa. It is my understanding that Joey Glimco has been many a year since he was convicted of some sort of a crime. I don't know exactly what it was. But on the other charges against him, either he was found innocent by the jury or the cases were dropped; isn't that correct?

Mr. Kennedy. He is one of the close associates of Tony Accardo. Paul "The Waiter" Ricca, the leading gangsters in Chicago, and has been identified before this committee and other public bodies for years as being a close associate of these people. He has 30 arrests. And he has a number of convictions.

Mr. Hoffa. Our constitution does not deal with associations, but deals with the operation of a union.

Mr. Kennedy. That would be fine. Then you get back and you say that the man has to be convicted. Then we give you the example of Glenn Smith, who says he took $20,000 of union funds to make a payoff, and you have not taken any action against him. You have the fellow in Minneapolis, Ray Brennan, who appealed all the way to the Supreme Court. He is still in office. You have not taken any action against him, and that is in the Central Conference of Teamsters. And Jorgensen and Williams, all three of them are union officials in Minneapolis, all have taken appeals to the Supreme Court. No action has been taken against them, has it, Mr. Hoffa?

Mr. Hoffa. There has been no action taken against Jorgensen or Brennan. It is my understanding that Jorgensen's membership, he went in front of them, took his case there, they reaffirmed their desire to have him represent them, and I believe, from the information that we have, although I do not have it in writing, that Brennan did the same thing.

I think the membership has a right to select the people they want to represent them. In due time, all those cases will be handled and investigated under the constitution.

Mr. Kennedy. What about Mr. Frank Matulla, out in California?

Mr. Hoffa. What about him?

Mr. Kennedy. He has been convicted of perjury.

Mr. Hoffa. Frank Matulla is up on appeal. I have taken no action.

Mr. Kennedy. Have you made any charges against him?

Mr. Hoffa. I have not.

Mr. Kennedy. Have you suspended him?
Mr. Hoffa. I have not.

Mr. Kennedy. He has been convicted of perjury. Bernie Adelstein, have you taken any action against Adelstein in New York City?

Mr. Hoffa. I understand Adelstein has been indicted and I believe he is pending trial.

Mr. Kennedy. We had a good deal of information about him before the committee, about Bernie Adelstein. Did you look into any of that?

Mr. Hoffa. I did not. I have not had an opportunity.

Mr. Kennedy. He is a close associate of Toney "Ducks" Corallo, Nick Ratteni, well-known gangsters in the United States. Why is it in every section of the country these people exist, Mr. Hoffa, in the Teamsters Union, and you have not taken any action against any of them? You have not taken any action against Bernie Adelstein?

Mr. Hoffa. I said I didn't.

Mr. Kennedy. You have Roland McMasters out in Detroit. Does he work for you?

Mr. Hoffa. What did he do so bad?

Mr. Kennedy. Does he work for you?
Mr. Hoffa. He does, local 299, my own local union.

Mr. Kennedy. How long has he been with you?

Mr. Hoffa. I believe Mac came with us somewhere around the 1940's.

Mr. Kennedy. Did you write a letter for him to obtain a deferment from the draft for him?

Mr. Hoffa. I probably did, if he requested it. He was still inducted. As you know, he has one bad eye.

Mr. Kennedy. Did you say he was essential for the work there in local 299?

Mr. Hoffa. Yes.

Mr. Kennedy. At the same time you wrote the letter, was he under indictment on a charge of felonious assault against Leslie Smith and Brother Hugh Smith, these two brothers being assaulted with baseball bats and knives?

Mr. Hoffa. I don't remember if he was or not. I don't remember the indictment.

Mr. Kennedy. Here is the letter that you wrote, and I quote: You described his activities : Settling of all labor disputes between management and labor and particularly through his extensive knowledge was very successful in the careful handling of all jurisdictional disputes between various A. F. of L. labor organizations; also with the CIO, in particular of keeping a continuous supply of essential war materials flowing into our war industries.

Mr. Williams. If you are going to ask him questions about a letter, may we see the letter, please?

The Chairman. The Chair presents to you the letter the counsel has referred to. You may examine it and identify it, please.

(The document was handed to the witness.)

(The witness conferred with his counsel.)

The Chairman. Do you identify the letter, Mr. Hoffa?

Mr. Hoffa. I beg your pardon, sir.

The Chairman. Do you identify the letter?

Mr. Hoffa. I must have sent this. It is back to January 5, 1943. I don't remember it, but my signature is on it. It does not look as though — when I say my signature, my name is on it. It does not look as though it is my signature. It could very well be. It could have been one of my secretaries or somebody else signed it with my permission.

The Chairman. All right. It may be made exhibit 19.

Mr. Kennedy. It says in the letter that McMasters was promoted to the position of "paid business representative on December 19, 1941". At that time he was under indictment, at the time that you promoted him to paid business representative.

Mr. Williams. Where is that, Mr. Kennedy?

Mr. Kennedy. The bottom of the first page.

(At this point, Senator Goldwater entered the hearing room.)

Mr. Kennedy. Prior to that, in the 1930's, he had 2 other convictions, Mr. Hoffa, 1 for assault and battery, and 1 for larceny of auto tires in 1932.

Senator John F. Kennedy. Mr. Hoffa, you say you wrote the letter in 1943?

Mr. Hoffa. The letter seems as though I did.

Senator John F. Kennedy. What was your job?

Mr. Hoffa. President of local 299.

Senator John F. Kennedy. Well, now, what was your status? This was in regard to the draft?

Mr. Hoffa, That is right.

Senator John F. Kennedy. What was your status?

Mr. Hoffa. I believe I was 1-A.

Senator John F. Kennedy. Were you called up?

Mr. Hoffa. No, sir.

Senator John F. Kennedy. For what reason?

Mr. Hoffa. Did you say for what reason?

Senator John F. Kennedy. Yes.

Mr. Hoffa. I assume the fact that I was in transportation.

Senator John F. Kennedy. Did Mr. Bennett write a letter for you?

Mr. Hoffa. I think he must have.

Senator John F. Kennedy. You must know about that. That would be fairly important, wouldn't it?

Mr. Hoffa. Well, I probably had a letter drafted, I don't recall exactly what Brennan wrote, but he must have had a letter drafted asking for deferment.

Senator John F. Kennedy. Did you ask him about the letter?

Mr. Hoffa. I did. I am quite sure I did.

Senator John F. Kennedy. Mr. Ray Bennett, what was his position at that time?

Mr. Hoffa. I would think he would be international organizer.

Senator John F. Kennedy. And he was in the picture, identified as a member of the bomb squad?

Mr. Hoffa. He was picked up.

Senator John F. Kennedy. As being a member of the bomb squad?

Mr. Hoffa. I don't know if they listed him as that, as such.

Senator John F. Kennedy. You saw this picture that was put in as an exhibit?

Mr. Hoffa. No, I did not see the picture, Senator Kennedy.

Senator John F. Kennedy. I am sorry. Anyway, you know who Mr. Bennett is?

Mr. Hoffa. Yes, I do.

(The photograph was handed to the witness.)

Senator John F. Kennedy. He wrote the letter in 1943?

Mr. Hoffa. I believe I requested a letter to be drafted.

Senator John F. Kennedy. He wrote it, in answer to your request?

(The witness conferred with his counsel.)

Mr. Hoffa. I beg your pardon, what did you say?

Senator John F. Kennedy. He wrote the letter, then, in answer to your request in 1943, is that correct?

Mr. Hoffa. If he wrote the letter, I probably requested him.

Senator John F. Kennedy. Do you know what was the result of the letter.

Mr. Hoffa. I was not inducted.

Senator John F. Kennedy. Who wrote one for him?

Mr. Hoffa. Well, I wouldn't know offhand. I don't remember. I think he was the age he probably would not have been drafted.

The following pages are excerpts of the transcripts from Russell Bufalino's testimony at the McClellan Hearings. He was one of many Cosa Nostra members that would invoke the Fifth Amendment for just about every question asked by chief counsel Robert Kennedy.

MONDAY, JUNE 30, 1958

United States Senate, Select Committee on Improper Activities, in the Labor or Management Field, Washington, D. C.

Present: Senator John L. McClellan, Democrat, Arkansas; Senator Irving M. Ives, Republican, New York; **Senator John F. Kennedy**, Democrat, Massachusetts; Senator Sam J. Ervin, Jr., Democrat, North Janetina; Senator Barry Goldwater, Republican, Arizona; Senator Karl E. Mundt, Republican, South Dakota.

Also present: **Robert F. Kennedy**, chief counsel; Paul J. Tierney, assistant counsel; John P. Constandy, assistant counsel; John J. McGovern, assistant counsel: Pierre E. G. Salinger, investigator; Walter R. May, investigator; George H. Martin, investigator; Sherman Willse, investigator; Ruth Young Watt, chief clerk.

TESTIMONY OF RUSSELL BUFALINO

The Chairman. State your name, your place of residence, and your business or occupation.

Mr. Bufalino. My name is Russell Bufalino. I reside at 304 East Dorrance Street, Kingston, Pa.

Mr. Agolino. Mr. Chairman, at this time I would like permission to address the chair.

The Chairman. Just one moment. I was trying to get the witness identified. I asked him about his business, profession, or occupation.

Did you answer that part of the question?

Mr. Bufalino. I respectfully decline to answer that question on the grounds it may tend to incriminate me.

The Chairman. Do you have counsel?

Mr. Bufalino. I do.

The Chairman. Counsel; identify yourself for the record, please.

Mr. Agolino. My name is Ettore S. Agolino, with offices in the Kehoe Building, Pittson, Pa.

The Chairman. Thank you very much. You say you have a brief statement you wish to make, Mr. Counsel?

Mr. Agolino. Yes, sir.

The Chairman. All right.

Mr. Agolino. Mr. Chairman. Russell Bufalino is at present a respondent in an action brought by the United States Immigration and Naturalization Service under deportation proceedings, and his case has not yet been disposed of. For this reason, he desires to avail himself of the privilege afforded him by the fifth amendment of the United States Constitution.

(Unless otherwise noted, Mr. Bufalino continued to invoke his fifth amendment right against self incrimination.)

The Chairman. All right. We understand that he will do that. You may proceed, Mr. Kennedy.

Mr. Kennedy (RFK): Would you tell me where you were born?

RFK. Mr. Bufalino, our interest in you centers around your attending the meeting at Apalachin and also your union contacts. I think that we have some information that would indicate that you played a very prominate role in setting up the meeting at Apalachin; that you did it with the assistance of Mr. Barbara. I wonder if you would make any comments on that before we start to develop the facts that we have.

RFK. According to our information, you were born on October 29, 1903, in Montedoro, Italy. That is in Sicily. Is that correct?

RFK. And yet despite that fact, the records at Luzerne County in Wilkes-Barre, Pa., show that you were born October 29, 1903, in Pittston Township, Pa.

RFK. Could you explain to the committee how it is that these records show that you were born in Pittston, Pa., when, in fact, you were born in Italy?

RFK. Is Mary Bufalino any relation to you?

RFK. Isn't it a fact that Mary Bufalino worked in the records office in Wilkes-Barre, Pa?

RFK. Are you related to Mr. William Bufalino?

RFK. Isn't it correct that William Bufalino, who is secretary-treasurer of Local 985 of the Teamsters, is a cousin of yours?

RFK. Isn't it correct also that Mr. William Bufalino is an attorney?

RFK. Did Mr. William Bufalino play any part in altering the records at the Wilkes-Barre Records Office?

.RFK. Wasn't it the purpose of getting the records altered so that it would appear that you were born here in the United States, and, therefore, could not be deported to Italy.

RFK. Can you tell us what companies you own or operate in the Pittston-Wilkes-Barre-Scranton area?

RFK. Do you own and operate the Penn Drape & Curtain Co., of South Main Street, Pittston, Pa.?

RFK. Are the Sciandras of Pittston, Pa., in business with you?

RFK. What was your wife's maiden name?

Mr. Bufalino. Janetina Sciandra.

RFK. Isn't it a fact that Angelo Sciandra attended the meeting at Apalachin?

RFK. Could you tell us if you have ever been arrested, Mr. Bufalino?

RFK. Isn't it a fact that you have been arrested some 7 or 8 times?

RFK. And that you have not been convicted on any of those charges?

RFK. We have a number of companies with whom we believe you are connected, starting with the ABS Contracting Co., of Pittston, Pa. Is it correct that you are associated with them?

RFK. The Penn Drape & Curtain Co., in Pittston, Pa.?
Mr. Bufalino. The same answer.

RFK. Would you answer the question?

RFK. And you were associated with Bonnie Stewart, Inc., of New York City, N. Y.

RFK. Isn't it correct that Dominic Alaimo and James Plumeri both had financial interests in that company also?

RFK. And Claudia Frocks of 224 West 35th Street, New York?

RFK. Isn't it correct that Angelo Sciandra also has an interest in that company?

RFK. And isn't it correct also that he pays you a certain amount of money each week for the work that you do for that company?

RFK. You are on the payroll as an expediter. Could you tell us what an expediter does?

DIGGING FOR THE TRUTH

RFK. Do you in fact do any work for this company, or are you on the payroll because of your connections, Mr. Bufalino?

RFK. You receive from that company $105 a week gross, is that right?

RFK. And you were put on the payroll back in 1953, were you not?

RFK. Then also you are on the payroll of the Fair Frox as an expediter. You are on their payroll also?

RFK. That is F-a-i-r F-r-o-x, and you are on their pay- roll as expediter at $125 a week, are you not?

RFK. Could you tell us what you do to earn that money?

RFK. Isn't it a fact that part of the money you receive is to handle labor relations for those companies, and to prevent any trouble difficulties with the union?

RFK. Aren't you able to do that because of the contacts and associates that you have, Mr. Bufalino?

RFK. And they include such people, do they not, as Johnny Dioguardi?

RFK. John Ormento?

RFK. Nig Rosen?

RFK. Dominick Alaimo?

RFK. John Charles Montana?

RFK. Vito Genovese?

RFK. James A. Osticco?

RFK. Frank Carbo?

RFK. James Plumeri?

RFK. Thomas Lucchese?

RFK. We have telephone calls from you, Mr. Bufalino, to L. G. Carriers, which is James Plumeri's company.

Could you tell us what you discussed with them?

RFK. What do you discuss with Charles Bufalino?

RFK. The Tri-City Dress Co., owned by Anthony Guarneri, can you tell us about that?

RFK. The Vic Vera Sportswear Co., New York City, which is owned and operated by a close friend of James Plumeri?

RFK. Isn't it a fact that James Plumeri set this lady up in the Vic Vera Sportswear Co.?

RFK. And Harvic Sportswear, of Scranton, Pa. Can you tell us what you called them about?

RFK. That is a shop, is it not, that is owned by Thomas Lucchese?

RFK. Have you also had other sources of income from gambling, Mr. Bufalino?

RFK. You have taken a great interest in basketball games, have you not?

RFK. And when you go to New York, you stay at the Hotel Forrest in New York City, is that correct, Mr. Bufalino?

RFK. Why is it that you and the individuals with police records very often stay at the Hotel Forrest in New York City?

RFK. Isn't it correct that you arranged with Mr. Barbara to set up the meeting at Apalachin in November 1957?

RFK. Isn't it correct that you were talking by telephone with Mr. Barbara frequently just prior to the meeting at Apalachin?

RFK. According to the information that we have, you made long distance telephone calls to Barbara on June 8, 11, 23, two on the 28th, July 23, July 27, September 4, September 11, September 12,

October 6, October 13, and October 26, is that correct?

RFK. And he called you on June 5, 10, 24, July 20, August 9, and October 23?

RFK. And isn't it correct that you in fact made hotel reservations for some of these individuals attending the meeting at Apalachin?

RFK. Isn't it a fact that you made a hotel reservation at the Casey Hotel in Scranton, Pa. for November 13, 1957?

RFK. And you made hotel reservations for an individual by the name of J. Cerrito, of Los Gatos, Calif.?

RFK. And that another reservation for the same night was made for J. Civello of Dallas, Tex.?

RFK. And this individual did, in fact, attend the meeting at Apalachin, is that correct.

RFK. And Scozzari, from San Gabriel, Calif.?

RFK. While he was there, Mr. Scozzari put in two telephone calls to you, isn't that correct?

RFK. And isn't is a fact that Mr. Scozzari attended the meeting at Apalachin?

DIGGING FOR THE TRUTH

RFK. And Frank DeSimone, you also made a reservation for him.

RFK. Mr. Scozzari, when he was arrested, or stopped by the police, had $10,000 on him, but listed himself as unemployed.

Can you give us any explanation for that?

RFK. All these hotel reservations that were made for these 5 individuals, of which we can show that 3 actually attended the meeting in Apalachin, were all charged to you personally, isn't that correct, Mr. Bufalino?

RFK. Did these other two individuals, Lanza and Scozzari, attend the meeting but were not caught?

RFK. When you came to the meeting, you came, did you not, with DeSimone, Civello and Scozzari?

RFK. That automobile that you drove was owned by William Medico, was it not?

RFK. And he owns the Medico Electric Motor Co. in Pittsburgh, Pa J.

RFK. Excuse me. That should be in Pittston, Pa. He owns the Medico Electric Motor Co. in Pittston. does he not?

RFK. This is the same individual that Mr. Montana stated that he was driving down to see, to find out how his compressor was coming?

RFK. And you in fact were driving an automobile belonging to one of his companies up to the meeting at Apalachin, were you not?

RFK. At the time that the New York State troopers checked your car, you had Vito Genovese with you, did you not?

RFK. Gerardo Cateno?

RFK. Dominick Olivetto?

RFK. And Joseph Ida?

RFK. And you stayed, when you were in Binghamton in March— you made another visit to Joseph Barbara in March 1957, did you not, Mr. Bufalino?

RFK. And at that time, you were with Vincenzo Osticco? Isn't that right?

RFK. And also with you was Angelo Sciandra, and you stayed at the Arlington Hotel, in Binghamton, N. Y.?

RFK. And the bill was charged to the Canada Dry Beverage Co., of Endicott, N.Y., was it not?

DIGGING FOR THE TRUTH 215

RFK. What were you there for? What business were you there on?

RFK. Do you know how your cousin, William Bufalino, was made head of Local 985 of the Teamsters?

RFK. Do you know Mr. James Hoffa?

RFK. Do you know Mr. Santo Volpe, from Pennsylvania?

RFK. Mr. Chairman, we consider that this individual is a very important figure. He has a number of the dress companies that operate in Pennsylvania. He also played an important role in the labor negotiations that took place at the beginning of this year. He is a close associate of Mr. Chair and it would appear that he was the one, together with Barbara, who set up and made the appointments and arrangements for setting up the meeting at Apalachin. He is a man of considerable importance and a man of great contacts throughout the United States and the underworld.

The Chairman. Do you want to comment upon those statements?

The Chairman. Is there anything further?

Have you any questions, Senator?

Senator Mundt. I have no questions.

The Chairman. Stand aside.

Call the next witness.

RFK. Thomas Lucchese.

The Chairman. Just one moment, please. The witness will continue under the same subpoena, subject to being recalled, if and whenever the committee desires to further interrogate him. If you will acknowledge the recognzance so to appear

Mr. Bufalino. Yes, sir.

The Chairman. Reasonable notice, of course, will be given to you.

Mr. Bufalino. O. K. Thank you.

The Chairman. Proceed, Mr. Kennedy.

The next section is the actual appeal from Tony Giacalone's son Joseph, attempting to take possession of his car that Charles "Chuckie" O'Brien borrowed to transport Hoffa to the Beaverland Street house in Detroit on July 30 1975.

UNITED STATES of America, Appellant, Plaintiff-Appellant,

v.

Joseph GIACALONE and One 1975 Mercury Four-Door Automobile, Maroon In Color, Bearing License Plate Number TMS 416, Appellee, Defendant-Appellee.

No. 75-2121.

United States Court of Appeals, Sixth Circuit.

Argued Oct. 15, 1975.

Decided Aug. 18, 1976.

Frederick S. Van Tiem, U. S. Atty., Robert C. Ozer, C. Stanley Hunterton, Detroit Strike Force, Detroit, Mich., for the U. S.

N. C. DeDay LaRene, Detroit, Mich., for Giacalone.

Before PHILLIPS, Chief Judge, and WEICK, EDWARDS, * CELEBREZZE, PECK, McCREE, LIVELY and ENGEL, Circuit Judges, sitting en banc.

WEICK, Circuit Judge.

The Government has appealed from an order of the United States District Court for the Eastern

District of Michigan granting a motion for return of seized property under Fed.R.Crim.P. 41(e). The seized property consisted of an automobile and its contents belonging to Joseph Giacalone. The automobile and contents were seized by the FBI pursuant to a search warrant issued by a United States Magistrate. The District Court held that the affidavit for the warrant submitted to the Magistrate did not allege sufficient facts to support the Magistrate's finding of probable cause. It granted the motion and ordered the automobile and contents returned to Giacalone. The Government seeks a reversal of that judgment. We reverse.

A temporary stay of the order of the District Court was granted by a Judge of this Court and it was later extended to run pending the appeal.

The affidavit for the warrant reads as follows:
JAMES C. ESPOSITO, being duly sworn according to law, deposes and states as follows:
I am a Special Agent of the FBI and I have been engaged since August 3, 1975, in an investigation into the disappearance and possible abduction of JAMES R. HOFFA (hereafter HOFFA).
The FBI has been informed by JAMES P. HOFFA, the son of HOFFA, that on July 30, 1975, and for some time prior thereto, HOFFA was engaged in a highly publicized campaign, to express his views and opinions in support of his own nomination and candidacy for the office of President of the International Brotherhood of Teamsters (IBT) a labor organization as defined by Section 152 of Title 29, United States Code. On July 30, 1975, HOFFA left his home in Lake Orion, Michigan,

and traveled to the Machus Red Fox restaurant at Maple and Telegraph Roads in Bloomfield Township, Michigan, and he advised witnesses, who have in turn advised the FBI, the (sic) he intended to meet with ANTHONY GIACALONE and ANTHONY PROVENZANO. At approximately 2:30 p. m., July 30, 1975, HOFFA telephoned his wife and advised her that GIACALONE had not as yet arrived at the Red Fox for the said meeting. No member of HOFFA's family has seen him or heard from him since that time.

JAMES P. HOFFA has advised the FBI that HOFFA, his father, was definitely conscious of the possibility of physical harm from opponents of his in the labor movement and that HOFFA, as of July 30, 1975, was a member of the IBT. JAMES P. HOFFA has stated to the FBI that CHARLES L. J. O'BRIEN (O'BRIEN) is one of the small number of persons with whom HOFFA is acquainted and with whom HOFFA would willingly enter an automobile. JAMES P. HOFFA has advised the FBI that this is so notwithstanding the fact that O'BRIEN, who was raised in the HOFFA home as a son of HOFFA, has during the past several months aligned himself with ANTHONY GIACALONE with whom O'BRIEN has actively supported HOFFA's opponents and enemies in the labor movement. O'BRIEN is currently employed by the IBT at the pleasure of HOFFA's opponents in office.

As part of the FBI investigation during the past week, witnesses have advised the FBI that

O'BRIEN vigorously claimed and insisted that at the time of HOFFA's disappearance during the afternoon of July 30, 1975, he (O'BRIEN) was with ANTHONY GIACALONE at the Southfield Athletic Club. Various witnesses, including the owner of the Southfield Athletic Club have denied that O'BRIEN was ever there on July 30, 1975.

On August 6, 1975, O'BRIEN admitted to Special Agents of the FBI that he (O'BRIEN), on July 30, 1975, borrowed from JOSEPH GIACALONE, a 1975 4-door Mercury Brougham automobile, maroon in color, which he (O'BRIEN) used to deliver a 40 pound frozen salmon to Mrs. ROBERT HOLMES, SR. in Farmington, Michigan, sometime between 12:00 p. m. and 1:00 p. m., and that he thereafter had the said automobile washed, O'BRIEN claimed, because blood from the salmon had stained the seat. Extensive interviews by the FBI have failed to identify anyone who has seen O'BRIEN during the period of approximately 2:20-2:30 p. m. on July 30, 1975, until "late afternoon" July 30, 1975, which is the only approximation that JOSEPH GIACALONE was able to provide to Special Agents of the FBI with respect to the time that day that O'BRIEN returned the automobile to GIACALONE.

The office of the Michigan Secretary of State has advised the FBI that there is listed as registered to Liftall Company, 2679 Conner, Detroit, Michigan, a 1975 Mercury four door automobile, license tag 1975 Michigan TMS 416. JOSEPH GIACALONE was interviewed on August 8, 1975, and acknowledged that he is the owner of Liftall Company and that he (JOSEPH GIACALONE) is the owner of the said 1975 Mercury 4-door automobile bearing license tag TMS 416. JOSEPH GIACALONE is known to me to be the son of ANTHONY GIACALONE.

JOSEPH GIACALONE was requested by Special Agents of the FBI, on August 8, 1975, to voluntarily permit a search of the said automobile for any evidence of fingerprints or microscopic particles of blood, hair, clothing, fibers, or flesh which can be identified as that of a human being, or specifically as that of HOFFA, as well as any physical evidence indicating where the automobile has been. Counsel of JOSEPH GIACALONE has (informed) the FBI that no inspection of JOSEPH GIACALONE'S automobile will be permitted, except pursuant to a search and seizure warrant.

For all of the above reasons I feel that probable cause exists to believe that CHARLES O'BRIEN has used JOSEPH GIACALONE's automobile to facilitate an abduction of HOFFA; and that the said abduction constitutes the use of force and violence to restrain, interfere, and prevent HOFFA from exercising his rights to which he is entitled under Section 411, Title 29, United States Code; and that evidence of the said abduction, to wit, fingerprints and microscopic particles of blood, clothing, fibers, flesh, and hair which can be identified as that of a human being, or specifically that of HOFFA, as well as any physical evidence indicating where the automobile has been, is being concealed on the said 1975 4-door Mercury automobile, maroon in color, bearing license tag number TMS 416 registered to Liftall Company.

I represent that it is necessary to seize the said automobile as soon as it may be found, at any time during the day or night, in order to minimize the time during which evidence contained therein may be disturbed, deliberately or otherwise, now that JOSEPH GIACALONE is aware of FBI interest in that automobile. The FBI is currently unaware of the location of the said automobile although a search for it is in progress.

/s/ JAMES C. ESPOSITO
/s/ Special Agent, FBI
Subscribed and Sworn to Before Me
this 8th Day of August, 1975.
/s/ BARBARA K. HACKETT
U. S. Magistrate

Before addressing the sufficiency of the affidavit we must examine the threshold question of mootness raised by appellee. This issue arose because a Grand Jury, which was investigating the disappearance of Mr. Hoffa and possible violations of federal law, issued a subpoena duces tecum for the automobile and it was served by the United States Marshal on the defendant after the District Court had entered its order for the return of the automobile to him. The order of the District Court had been stayed by this Court and the appeal ordered expedited. The purpose of the subpoena duces tecum is not clear to us as it would seem that the Government was adequately protected by our stay.

The theory for the subpoena duces tecum was that Giacalone had constructive possession of the automobile because of the order of the District Court even though it had been stayed. Enforcement of the subpoena duces tecum was procured in the District Court where Giacalone was charged with contempt for refusing to surrender his constructive possession, and finally he did surrender his constructive possession of the automobile in order to purge himself from the contempt. By reason of this unnecessary procedure a new issue was injected in this case, and it has delayed consideration of the appeal.

Giacalone argues that we should dismiss this appeal as moot; however, the granting of a Rule 41(e) motion serves not only to restore possession of seized property to its owner, but also serves as a ruling that the search and seizure of the property were illegal, and that the fruits of the search "shall not be admissible in evidence at any hearing or trial." Because the District Court's ruling will be binding on all courts in future criminal litigation, the consequences of the ruling reach beyond the issue of custody of the car; furthermore, this binding effect on future litigation requires that we review the ruling at this time rather than hold that the question is not ripe because Giacalone has not yet been indicted.

Turning to the affidavit for the warrant, we must confront the problem of defining what allegations are necessary therein to support a finding of probable cause. Most of the major pronouncements of the Supreme Court in recent years on the subject discuss the sufficiency of certain classes of allegations in affidavits. 1

During the early years of the Constitution the Supreme Court did not seem troubled by the meaning of probable cause; Chief Justice Marshall wrote:

(Probable cause) has a fixed and well-known meaning. It imports a seizure made under circumstances which warrant suspicion.

Locke v. United States, 11 U.S. (7 Cranch) 339, 348, 3 L.Ed. 364 (1813).

Today more than suspicion is required, Brinegar v. United States, 338 U.S. 160, 175, 69 S.Ct. 1802, 93 L.Ed. 1879 (1949), because the word "suspicion" in its present usage would seem to permit a search upon a hunch. 2 The Court in Brinegar also stated that a showing of probable cause was unlike a showing of guilt:

There is a large difference between the two things to be proved (guilt and probable cause), as well as between the tribunals which determine them, and therefore a like difference in the quanta and modes of proof required to establish them. (338 U.S. at 173, 69 S.Ct. at 1309)

Brinegar thus teaches that probable cause is a showing of more than suspicion but less than guilt.

Aguilar v. Texas, 378 U.S. 108, 114, 84 S.Ct. 1509, 1514, 12 L.Ed.2d 723 (1964), the Court made a further comment on the required contents of an affidavit, holding:

(T)he magistrate must be informed of some of the underlying circumstances from which the informant concluded that the narcotics were where he claimed they were.

While Aguilar dealt with the necessity of showing grounds for believing hearsay given by an unnamed informant, the requirement that a warrant state "some of the underlying circumstances" supporting the affiant's belief was adopted in reviewing an affidavit without the unnamed informant problem United States v. Ventresca, 380 U.S. 102, 85 S.Ct. 741, 13 L.Ed.2d 684 (1965). There the Court observed that the affidavit being reviewed contained "not merely 'some of the underlying circumstances' supporting the officer's belief, but a good many of them". Id. at 109, 85 S.Ct. at 746.

Thus, after Ventresca it is apparent that an affidavit is sufficient if it shows some of the underlying circumstances supporting the affiant's belief which could lead a man of reasonable caution 3 to conclude that evidence that a federal crime had been committed will probably be found in the place sought to be searched.

United States v. Harris, 403 U.S. 573, 581, 91 S.Ct. 2075, 29 L.Ed.2d 723 (1971), and Rugendorf v. United States, 376 U.S. 528, 533, 84 S.Ct. 825, 11 L.Ed.2d 887 (1964), and Jones v. United States, 362 U.S. 257, 271, 80 S.Ct. 725, 4 L.Ed.2d 697 (1960), the Court, in approving findings of probable cause, stated that there was a substantial basis in the affidavits for the findings. This language should not be construed to establish a " substantial evidence" standard of review as used by a court in reviewing the sufficiency of evidence in a criminal trial. Because substantial evidence is all that is required to support a verdict of guilty, and because a showing of probable cause requires less than a showing of guilt, it appears that a substantial basis exists when the affidavit shows some underlying circumstances which could lead a man of reasonable caution to conclude that evidence of a federal crime will probably be found in the place to be searched. The ambiguity of the "substantial basis" language in those decisions leads us to conclude that the phrase is a substitute term for the "underlying circumstances" test set out above.

This Circuit has consistently held that once a Magistrate has found probable cause and has issued a warrant, his judgment is conclusive unless arbitrarily exercised, since the purpose of the Fourth Amendment has been served by his review of the affidavit. United States v. Arms, 392 F.2d 300, 302 (6th Cir. 1968); United States v. Jordan, 349 F.2d 107, 108 (6th Cir. 1965); United States v. Haskins, 345 F.2d 111, 113 (6th Cir. 1965); United States v. Nicholson, 303 F.2d 330, 332 (6th Cir.), cert. denied, 371 U.S. 823, 83 S.Ct. 43, 9 L.Ed.2d 63 (1962); Evans v. United States, 242 F.2d 534, 536 (6th Cir.), cert. denied, 353 U.S. 976, 77 S.Ct. 1059, 1 L.Ed.2d 1137 (1957).

The purpose of the probable cause requirement is not so much to establish a burden of proof as to require that searches be authorized by an impartial judicial officer. As stated in the often quoted passage Johnson v. United States, 333 U.S. 10, 13-14, 68 S.Ct. 367, 369, 92 L.Ed. 436 (1948):

The point of the Fourth Amendment, which often is not grasped by zealous officers, is not that it denies law enforcement the support of the usual inferences which reasonable men draw from evidence. Its protection consists in requiring that those inferences be drawn by a neutral and detached magistrate instead of being judged by the officer engaged in the often-competitive enterprise of ferreting out crime.

Thus, warrants are not to be read in a negative or hyper technical manner, and great deference is to be given to the Magistrate's decision. United States v. Ventresca, 380 U.S. at 109, 85 S.Ct. 741.

A further reason for avoiding a hyper technical or rigorous standard for reviewing a search warrant is that a finding of insufficiency of an affidavit leads to suppression of evidence. The suppression of evidence seized pursuant to a search warrant should not be treated lightly; in suppressing evidence the truth is suppressed, and an investigation into a crime is impeded. McCray v. Illinois, 386 U.S. 300, 307, 87 S.Ct. 1056, 18 L.Ed.2d 62 (1967).

Finally, the need to interpret affidavits in a "common-sense and realistic fashion" is mandated by the fact that warrants are often sought on short notice for the purpose of preventing the destruction of evidence, and because, as stated United States v. Ventresca, 380 U.S. at 108, 85 S.Ct. at 746.

(Affidavits) are normally drafted by nonlawyers in the midst and haste of a criminal investigation. Technical requirements of elaborate specificity once exacted under common law pleadings have no proper place in this area.

In reviewing this affidavit the District Court stated two elements of proof which it found lacking and which it believed were necessary to establish probable cause. The Court stated first that it was necessary to show proof that the motive behind Hoffa's alleged abduction was to deny him his rights as a member of the Teamsters' Union, and second, that it was necessary to show proof that the automobile was used to abduct him. The problem with the District Court's position is that proof of the crime is supposed to be the result of a search, not a required precondition of the search. Deficiencies such as these might be significant in a criminal trial, or if the District Court were making a de novo determination of probable cause, but that determination was to be made by the Magistrate and not by the District Court.

In giving the Magistrate's judgment great deference, which the law requires even in a doubtful case, it is not the function of a reviewing court to state what elements of proof the Magistrate must consider indispensable in making his determination. There are no technical rules establishing a quantum of evidence necessary to support a finding of probable cause, nor are there rules requiring that the elements of a crime, or the sequential events of a crime, must be shown. The purpose of the reviewing court's inquiry is merely to determine from the facts set forth in the affidavit and the permissible inferences to be drawn there from whether the Magistrate's decision to issue the warrant was arbitrary because the affidavit contained no information which, if credited, was sufficient to establish probable cause. 4 These facts and the "common sense" inferences which can be drawn therefrom (see Ventresca, 380 U.S. at 108, 85 S.Ct. 741) are discussed below.

Here, the affidavit for the warrant stated that Mr. Hoffa "was definitely conscious of the possibility of physical harm" from his union opponents. Such action would violate federal law.

On the afternoon of Hoffa's disappearance he went to meet with at least one of his opponents. 5 Another union opponent, who was one of a very few persons with whom Hoffa would willingly enter an automobile, borrowed a car from the son of the opponent whom Hoffa was to meet, and then disappeared. Three hours after Hoffa was last heard from this union opponent reappeared, having had the interior of the borrowed car cleaned to remove bloodstains. His alibi was flimsy at best. 6 He failed to explain satisfactorily his own whereabouts after the time when Hoffa was last heard from. Hoffa had been missing for eight days when the affidavit for the warrant was filed. This was ample time to permit a foul-play inference which the Magistrate could properly draw.

These circumstances cannot be construed, just as easily, to support a finding that Hoffa took an unannounced vacation, or that he drove into the Michigan wilderness and committed suicide; rather, they clearly point to the probability that he was abducted in the automobile (here at issue) to prevent him from exercising his union rights. These circumstances would seem to call for a search of the automobile, and for a laboratory examination of its contents.

The FBI need not prove that Hoffa was abducted in order to procure a warrant to search the automobile; rather, it must search the automobile to obtain evidence that Hoffa was abducted.

None of the elements of the crime stated in 29 U.S.C. § 530 is conclusively established by this affidavit; however, we need only to look for facts supporting probabilities, for, as stated in Brinegar, 338 U.S. at 175, 69 S.Ct. at 1310, "in dealing with probable cause . . . we deal with probabilities."

The District Court ignored the evidence of probability appearing in this affidavit and the inferences properly deducible there from. The Court stated that the only evidence of interference with union rights was the statement that Hoffa was engaged in a struggle to regain the presidency of the union; but there is more. The affidavit implicates O'Brien, Joseph Giacalone and Anthony Giacalone, all of whom are connected with the Union and with opponents of Hoffa's campaign. Thus the very fact that they were involved is also an indication that the motive for the probable abduction was to prevent Hoffa's return to power in his union, a violation of federal law. To be sure, there are other possible explanations for the disappearance, but this motive virtually compels a finding of probability from the facts in the affidavit.

The District Court also dismissed the Government's claim as a mere theory, not proof. A theory is a hypothesis which is supported by some factual basis. In criminal cases the Court is required to instruct the jury on the theories of both the prosecution and the defense. The fact that the Government's theory had not yet been conclusively established does not negate a

finding of probable cause. Probable cause can arise from facts which create a theory of how the crime was committed. The very facts which transform a hypothesis into a theory also transform suspicion into probable cause. A theory itself becomes fact only when proven in a criminal trial to the satisfaction of the jury.

When an affidavit states facts upon which a reasonable man could conclude that a theory of a crime is probably correct, a Magistrate's finding of probable cause cannot be rejected as arbitrary. It is not necessary that a set of facts eliminate all but one possible explanation in order to establish probable cause, so long as the theory advanced in the affidavit appears to be probably correct.

Other federal courts have found support for probable cause when the nexus between the evidence sought and the place to be searched is arguably equivocal, as United States v. Mulligan, 488 F.2d 732 (9th Cir. 1973), cert. denied, 417 U.S. 930, 94 S.Ct. 2640, 41 L.Ed.2d 233 (1974); Edmondson v. United States, 402 F.2d 809 (10th Cir. 1968); and United States v. Scolnick, 392 F.2d 320 (3d Cir.), cert. denied sub nom. Brooks v. United States, 392 U.S. 931, 88 S.Ct. 2283, 20 L.Ed.2d 1389 (1968).

Similarly, probable cause for a policeman to make a warrantless arrest has been found in circumstances which arguably could support other explanations, as in Brinegar, supra, and Carroll v. United States, 267 U.S. 132, 45 S.Ct. 280, 69 L.Ed. 543 (1925). 7

The District Court also stated that one condition of Mr. Hoffa's parole was that he would not run for office in the union for a period of fifteen years. The fact that he was running for union office in violation of his parole is irrelevant to the question of probable cause because it was not mentioned in the affidavit.

When a court is faced with a situation wherein there is at issue the quantum of evidence necessary to be alleged to support a finding of probable cause, and when the affidavit arguably shows circumstances which could support a determination that evidence of a federal crime will probably be found in the place to be searched, the court should follow the practice expressed United States v. Lewis, 392 F.2d 377, 379 (2d Cir.), cert. denied, 393 U.S. 891, 89 S.Ct. 212, 21 L.Ed.2d 170 (1968): One of the best ways to foster increased use of warrants is to give law enforcement officials the assurance that when a warrant is obtained in a close case, its validity will be upheld.

We therefore apply the rule of United States v. Haskins, 345 F.2d 111, 113 (6th Cir. 1965), that the Magistrate's "determination is conclusive unless his judgment is arbitrarily exercised" and that there is "a presumption that a (Magistrate) has properly performed his duty."

Although the affidavit here is less than ideal, as was the affidavit United States v. Jenkins, 525 F.2d 819 (6th Cir. 1975), a doubtful case is to be "governed largely by the preference which our legal system gives to warrants." Id. at 824.

We find that the affidavit contains sufficient facts to indicate that the Magistrate's finding of probable cause was not arbitrary. The order of the District Court is reversed, and the Magistrate's finding of probable cause is affirmed.

LIVELY, Circuit Judge (concurring and dissenting) with whom Judges JOHN W. PECK and McCREE join.

I concur in the holding that this case is not moot, but respectfully dissent from the reversal of the judgment.

The judicial preference for warrants and for rules which encourage officers to seek them instead of conducting warrantless searches is universally recognized. Thus it has been held that the determination of an impartial magistrate on the issue of probable cause is entitled to "great deference". Spinelli v. United States,); United States v. Plemmons, 336 F.2d 731 (6 Cir. 1964) 393 U.S. 410, 419, 89 S.Ct. 584, 21 L.Ed.2d 637 (1969); Coury v. United States, 426 F.2d 1354, 1356 (6th Cir. 1970). However, such a determination is not conclusive, but is subject to review under standards which have been variously stated by this court. Evans v. United States, 242 F.2d 534, 536 (6th Cir.), cert. denied, 353 U.S. 976, 77 S.Ct. 1059, 1 L.Ed.2d 1137 (1957), we stated that the magistrate's determination of probable cause is "conclusive unless his judgment is arbitrarily exercised". United States v. Nicholson, 303 F.2d 330, cert. denied, 371 U.S. 823, 83 S.Ct. 43, 9 L.Ed.2d 63 (6 Cir. 1962; United States v. Gosser, 339 F.2d 102, cert. denied, 382 U.S. 819, 86 S.Ct. 44, 15 L.Ed.2d 66 (6 Cir. 1964); United States v. Jordan, 349 F.2d 107 (6 Cir. 1965); United States v. Arms, 392 F.2d 300 (6 Cir. 1968); DiPiazza v. United States, 415 F.2d 99 (6 Cir. 1969), cert. denied, 402 U.S. 949, 91 S.Ct. 1606, 29 L.Ed.2d 119 (1971).

The words "arbitrarily exercised" are not defined in our opinions. Jones v. United States, 362 U.S. 257, 80 S.Ct. 725, 4 L.Ed.2d 697 (1960), the Supreme Court, in confirming that an affidavit for a search warrant may be based on reliable hearsay rather than personal knowledge of the affiant, stated the test for a magistrate's determination of probable cause as follows:

But there was substantial basis for him to conclude that narcotics were probably present in the apartment, and that is sufficient. Id. at 271, 80 S.Ct. at 736.

Almost identical language was used Rugendorf v. United States, 376 U.S. 528, 533, 84 S.Ct. 825, 828, 11 L.Ed.2d 887 (1964), where the Court said We believe that there was substantial basis for the Commissioner to conclude that stolen furs were probably in the petitioner's basement. No more is required.

Aguilar v. Texas, 378 U.S. 108, 84 S.Ct. 1509, 12 L.Ed.2d 723 (1964), in dealing with the general standard of review the Court said, "Thus, when a search is based upon a magistrate's, rather than a police officer's determination of probable cause, the reviewing courts will accept evidence of a less 'judicially competent or persuasive character than would have justified an officer in acting on his own without a warrant,' Id. at 111, 84 S.Ct. at 1512 (quoting from Jones v. United States, supra, 362 U.S. at 270, 80 S.Ct. 725,) . . ." and then recited the language from Jones previously quoted which established the "substantial basis" test.

It thus appears that a reviewing court may not hold that a magistrate's judgment has been arbitrarily exercised if there is substantial basis for the magistrate to conclude that the property to be searched will probably produce evidence of the crime described by the one seeking the warrant. This is precisely what I find lacking in the affidavit in the present case. Though the affidavit recites an abundance of detail which formed the "underlying circumstances" that led the FBI agent to seek the warrant, it appears to me that a substantial basis for his conclusion that the automobile of Joseph Giacalone was involved in the disappearance of James R. Hoffa is lacking.

This conclusion that the affidavit is deficient does not result from a "hyper technical, rather than a commonsense" approach. Even conceding the probability that the unexplained disappearance of James R. Hoffa resulted from an abduction engineered by his enemies in the International Brotherhood of Teamsters, this is not enough. There must be some link between this assumed federal crime and the automobile of Joseph

Giacalone. When the affidavit is read as a whole it is clear that the activities of O'Brien on July 30, 1975 are relied upon to supply the connecting link. However, I find completely tenuous the conclusion that Charles O'Brien probably used the automobile of Joseph Giacalone to abduct James R. Hoffa. It is possible, of course, that this did occur, but the facts recited in the affidavit do not supply the probability that is required. Though O'Brien did borrow the automobile of Giacalone on the day of the disappearance, the affidavit fails to place O'Brien or the automobile at any place where Hoffa was said to be on that day. The government contends the magistrate could take judicial notice of the fact that Farmington, Michigan is about a ten-minute drive from the Machus Red Fox restaurant where Hoffa had gone. Nevertheless, the affidavit places O'Brien at Farmington between only 12:00 noon and 1:00 p. m., which was at least one and one-half hours before Hoffa disappeared. There is absolutely nothing to indicate that Hoffa and O'Brien were in the same vicinity after 2:30 p. m., when Hoffa was last heard from. The statement that the affiant "feels" that there is probable cause to believe that evidence consisting of fingerprints and microscopic particles of human blood, flesh, hair and clothing is being concealed on the automobile of Joseph Giacalone should properly be treated as a "mere conclusion," Aguilar v. Texas, 378 U.S. 108, 113, 84 S.Ct. 1509, 12 L.Ed.2d 723 (1964), or as a "mere affirmation of suspicion and belief." Nathanson v. United States, 290 U.S. 41, 46, 54 S.Ct. 11, 13, 78 L.Ed. 159 (1933).

I would affirm the judgment of the district court.

McCREE, Circuit Judge, with whom Judge PECK and Judge LIVELY join, (dissenting).

I concur in Judge Lively's dissenting opinion, and I write separately only because I was a member of the panel which decided one of the cases relied upon in the majority opinion for the proposition that "once a Magistrate has found probable cause and has issued a warrant, his judgment is conclusive unless arbitrarily exercised, since the purpose of the Fourth Amendment has been served by his review of the affidavit." The cited cases use the terms "abuse of discretion" and "arbitrariness" as a shorthand way of describing the courts' obligation to determine whether the facts in the affidavit and all the permissible inferences there from could afford the magistrate probable cause to believe that evidence of a crime would be found in the place to be searched. They do not hold that the magistrate's determination is "conclusive" and therefore immune from judicial review as suggested in the majority opinion.

Our precedents do not support the statement in the majority opinion that "the purpose of the Fourth Amendment has been served by (the magistrate's) review of the affidavit" and that "the purpose of the probable cause requirement is not so much to establish a burden of proof as to require that searches be authorized by an impartial judicial officer." The language of the Fourth Amendment explicitly rejects this analysis. It does not simply require that a warrant be judicially authorized. It also provides "no Warrants shall issue, but upon probable cause . . . ." This is an express requirement that the person seeking the issuance of a warrant must sustain the burden of affording the magistrate probable cause to believe that the place to be searched will produce the things to be seized. And probable cause means something more than reasonable suspicion. Terry v. Ohio, 392 U.S. 1, 88 S.Ct. 1868, 20 L.Ed.2d 889 (1968).

* Judge Edwards recused himself from the decision in this case.

1 Thus in Nathanson v. United States, 290 U.S. 41, 54 S.Ct. 11, 78 L.Ed. 159 (1933), the Court held insufficient an affidavit asserting only a suspicion or belief. Aguilar v. Texas, 378 U.S. 108, 84 S.Ct. 1509, 12 L.Ed.2d 723 (1964), an affidavit was held insufficient because it contained only conclusory statements. The Court dealt with the sufficiency of allegations based on hearsay from unnamed informants in several cases: United States v. Harris, 403 U.S. 573, 91 S.Ct. 2075, 29 L.Ed.2d 723 (1971); Spinelli v. United States, 393 U.S. 410, 89 S.Ct. 584, 21 L.Ed.2d 637 (1969); Rugendorf v. United States, 376 U.S. 528, 84 S.Ct. 825, 11 L.Ed.2d 887 (1964); Jones v. United States, 362 U.S. 257, 80 S.Ct. 725, 4 L.Ed.2d 697 (1960).

2 Brinegar involved a warrantless search. The Court in Nathanson v. United States, 290 U.S. 41, 47, 54 S.Ct. 11, 78 L.Ed. 159 (1933), held that a search warrant affidavit must contain more than a statement of mere suspicion and belief to support a finding of probable cause.

3 This objective "man of reasonable caution" standard is found in Brinegar v. United States, 338

U.S. at 175-76, 69 S.Ct. 1302, and Carroll v. United States, 267 U.S. 132, 162, 45 S.Ct. 280, 69 L.Ed. 543 (1925), and United States v. Nicholson, 303 F.2d 330, 332 (6th Cir.), cert. denied, 371 U.S. 823, 83 S.Ct. 43, 9 L.Ed.2d 63 (1962).

4 It appears that the difference between our view and that expressed in Judge Lively's dissent is not based upon different legal standards of review, but results from different conclusions as to what inferences can and should be drawn from the facts stated in the affidavit.

5 Unnamed witnesses informed the FBI that both Anthony Giacalone and Anthony Provenzano were to meet Hoffa. We recognize that this statement cannot support a finding of probable cause because the reliability of the witnesses has not been demonstrated; however, the affidavit also states that Hoffa's son said that Hoffa called home from the Machus Red Fox Restaurant and told his wife that Giacalone had not yet arrived. This statement is sufficient for purposes of a search warrant affidavit to establish the identity of the man whom Hoffa was to meet.

6 The Magistrate was entitled to consider the incredibility of the alibi. O'Brien told the FBI that he borrowed a friend's expensive, new automobile to deliver a huge fish to an acquaintance, and that blood from the fish stained the back seat of the automobile.

7 In Brinegar a heavily loaded car, driven by a suspected bootlegger, established probable cause to arrest, even though the heavy load could have been

caused by a number of lawful activities. Aguilar v. Texas, 378 U.S. at 111, 84 S.Ct. 1509, teaches that probable cause to issue a search warrant can be based on a standard of proof lower than the standard of proof for probable cause to justify a warrantless arrest.

Sources

The following books were referenced as well as newspaper articles from the *Detroit Free Press*, *Detroit News*, *Oakland Press*, *Toledo Blade*, *The Times Leader* of Wilkes-Barre Pennsylvania, *Associated Press*, *People Magazine*, and news broadcasts from *WJBK* Fox 2 Detroit, *WDIV*, Channel 4 Detroit, *WXYZ* Channel 7 Detroit, *Fox News Channel*, *NBC, CBS,* and *ABC News*. Information regarding Anthony Giacalone, Bagnasco Funeral Home, and Charles O'Brien was referenced from the Detroit Partnership webpage created by M. Flynt.

Asman, Charles. Sobel, Rebecca. *The Strange Disappearance of Jimmy Hoffa,* Manor Books, New York, 1976.

Brandt, Charles. *I Heard You Paint Houses: Frank "the Irishman" Sheeran and the inside story of the Mafia, the Teamsters, and the last ride of Jimmy Hoffa*, Hanover, NH: Steerforth Press, 2004, 2005.

Brill, Steven. *The Teamsters*. New York: Simon and Schuster, 1978

Davis, John H. *Mafia Kingfish: Carlos Marcello and the Assassination of John F. Kennedy*. New York: Signet, 1989.

Federal Bureau of Investigation Detroit Office HOFFEX Memo January 1976.

LaFontaine, Ray and Mary. *Oswald Talked*: The New Evidence in the JFK Assassination. Gretna, LA: Pelican Publishing, 1996.

Mass, Peter. *The Valachi Papers*. New York: Putnam, 1968.

Moldea, Dan E. *The Hoffa Wars: The Rise and Fall of Jimmy Hoffa*. New York: Shpolsky Publishers, 1978, 1993.

Posner, Gerald. *Case Closed: Lee Harvey Oswald and the Assassination of JFK*. New York: Anchor Books, 1993.

Russell, Thaddeus. *Out of the Jungle: Jimmy Hoffa and the remaking of the American working class*. New York: Knopf, 2001.

United States Court of Appeals, Sixth Circuit. Giacalone Vehicle Seizure Legal Brief. 1976.

United States, Investigation of Improper Activities in the Labor or Management Field 1957-1959 United States Senate, Washington D.C.

Zeller, Duke F.C. Devil's Pact: Inside the World of the Teamsters Union. Secaucus, N.J.: Birch Lane Press, 1996.

About the Author

Jeffry Scott Hansen was born in 1972 in the Brightmoor section of Northwest Detroit and graduated from Bishop Borgess High School in 1990. He joined the United States Marine Corps in 1991 and served honorably for four years.

In 2006, Mr. Hansen began collecting the information that would become the basis of this book. He is married with four daughters and currently a police officer in suburban Detroit.

Digging for the Truth: *The Final Resting Place of Jimmy Hoffa* is his third book.

Made in the USA